DO AMERICANS SHOP
TOO MUCH?

"New Democracy Forum operates at a level of literacy and responsibility which is all too rare in our time." —John Kenneth Galbraith

DO AMERICANS SHOP TOO MUCH?

JULIET SCHOR
FOREWORD BY RALPH NADER

EDITED BY JOSHUA COHEN AND JOEL ROGERS
FOR *BOSTON REVIEW*

BEACON PRESS
BOSTON

BEACON PRESS
25 Beacon Street
Boston, Massachusetts 02108-2892
www.beacon.org

Beacon Press books
are published under the auspices of
the Unitarian Universalist Association of Congregations.

06 05 04 03 02 01 00   8 7 6 5 4 3 2 1

This book is printed on recycled acid-free paper that contains at least 20
percent postconsumer waste and meets the uncoated paper ANSI/NISO
specifications for permanence as revised in 1992.

Composition by Wilsted & Taylor Publishing Services

Library of Congress Cataloging-in-Publication Data
Schor, Juliet.
    Do Americans shop too much? / Juliet Schor; foreword by
    Ralph Nader ; edited by Joshua Cohen and Joel Rogers for *Boston Review*.
        p. cm.
      ISBN 0-8070-0443-X (pbk.)
    1. Consumption (Economics)—United States.   2. Consumer behavior—
    United States.   3. Cost and standard of living—United States.
    I. Schor, Juliet.   II. Cohen, Joshua.   III. Rogers, Joel.

    HC110.C6 D6 2000
    339.4'7'0973—dc21

                                                    99-089273

CONTENTS

3

FOREWORD

RALPH NADER

In a country that respects "Shop till you drop" as the Eleventh Commandment, the politics and culture of consumption are vastly understudied. The exchange that follows is a welcome interruption of this striking silence. Simply by showing the possibility of some critical thinking about consumption, its contribution to public debate is assured.

Juliet Schor's lead essay, characteristically sharp and provocative, seeks to explain a "new consumerism," characterized by feverish upscaling of lifestyle expectations irrespective of personal means. This new consumerism features both mass desire for the "conspicuous consumption" that Thorstein Veblen once associated with the sumptuary rich, and mass frustration because such consumption is often out of reach. In Schor's view, an increasingly "competitive consumption"—a latter-day and much more aggressive version of "keeping up with the Joneses"—owes chiefly to increased income inequality and a vastly expanded frame of consumer comparison. The former requires those aspiring to emulate people one, two, or three rungs above them on the income ladder to reach higher, since the space between rungs has widened. The latter is due mainly to the increased reach of television and other media, which now broadcast the life-styles of the rich and famous into the homes and hearts of every social class, including the very poor. Coupled with the breakdown in neighborhood cohesiveness and the wholesale entry of women into the paid labor force, this broadcast of affluence has led aspiring consumers to shift their point of reference from their next-door neighbors—the "Joneses" of old, who were likely located in the same income group—to stylish representatives of increasingly remote upper-income groups.

As a friendly amendment to this explanation, I would add the contribution of the many marketing mavens—the consumer product companies, the Madison Avenue and London advertising firms, the new "permission marketing" consultants. After all, unless we believe (and neither Schor nor I do) that relentless status competition is deeply embedded in human nature, it does not follow automatically that increases in inequality, or even its relentless display, would lead to competitive consumption. Such conditions may provide the opportunity for "new consumerism," but it's the marketing folks who finally seize it. (In the exchange that follows, this view is effectively dismissed by Robert Frank on the grounds that advertising has been with us more or less forever. But while that's true, I think Frank may underappreciate the impact of recent changes in the capacity of the marketing machine.)

Part of the marketing effort is about targeting. On television, for example, with the decline in network viewership, both network and cable broadcasts now focus increasingly on specific demographic groups especially attractive to advertisers, for example, affluent young adults and children, with tailored programming to support the distorted inducements that Schor notes. On the Internet, detailed customer profiles, and specific pitches to individuals based on those profiles, are now essentially costless to assemble, and our toothless privacy laws have long assured more or less the same capacity to credit card companies of all kinds.

And part of it is just about scale. The credit card industry, for example, sends out 2.5 billion solicitations each year—advertisements that essentially urge consumers to spend, and promise them some help. Surely this level of solicitation has something to do with the sharp upsurge in credit card use in the last decade, and a concomitant run-up in consumer debt.

Most commonly, of course, it's about both. Consider the drug industry's investment in "direct-to-consumer" advertising, which rose from $25 million as recently as 1988 to more than $1 billion a decade later. The purpose of such advertising, which appears on television, in magazines, over the Internet, and in any other forum the industry can use, is to convince patients to badger their doctors to prescribe brand-name drugs, drugs that patients may not need, that may be unsafe, or for which there commonly are better or cheaper generic substitutes. Why this massive increase in advertising effort—unless those making it thought it positively affected sales?

Or, again, consider children, perhaps the group that most forcefully illustrates how truly pervasive, and malign, is today's hypercommercialism. Corporations today employ all sorts of marketing schemes, or commercial pressure on intermediaries (consider the efforts by Coke and Pepsi to gain exclusive beverage selling rights in schools), to bypass parents and sell directly to children. Focus groups and batteries of psychologists, teaming with schools to study buying and behavior habits, help get the message right. The extension of advertising into new realms—consider Channel 1's advertising, forced on about eight million captive youngsters daily, or Internet efforts to lure kids into a "flow state" of total absorption—helps put it across. The result of the marketing frenzy is that children are increasingly raised through an ever-widening blizzard of logo-featuring products, with the corporate product world crowding out and undermining both parental control and the emergence of the educated child. And make no mistake: this changes kids' behavior. The soft drink company efforts alone, for example, have fundamentally changed children's drinking habits. They now consume twice as much soda as they do milk, a reversal of the ratio of only two decades ago. And I very much doubt inner-city kids would be shooting themselves over high-priced footgear if they weren't relentlessly pummeled with the message that wearing it would somehow enable them to "be like Mike."

To be sure, debate about the roots of the new consumerism is bound to continue. In the meantime, there seems no dispute that the "new consumerism" is among us, and that its effects are largely malign. What to do about it? Among the contributors to this exchange, Juliet Schor, Betsy Taylor, and Douglas Holt all call for a revitalized consumer movement as a central element in a new politics of consumption. I join that call, but also urge that discussion move to the specific institutional forms such a movement might take. Granted that independent consumer organization is needed to raise new values, new ideas for policy to support their expression, and the political momentum to implement such policy, how do we get from here to there? No one knows precisely, and there is urgent need for experiment. Among some possibilities, however, I would encourage:

- Banding together for group buying in a community and/or through the Internet. Wholesale group-buying operations, where tens, hundreds, or thousands join together to negotiate bulk purchases and lower prices, now exist in patches around the country, especially in some insurance lines and home heating oil markets.

- Banding together for group information sharing and complaint handling. The Internet offers an excellent opportunity to create clearinghouses of consumer-generated information on product quality, defects, billing frauds, and so forth, with equally promising opportunities for victimized consumers to negotiate as a group for redress.

- Banding together for group negotiating. Voluntary, mass-based consumer policy organization could remake the terrain of consumer-seller interaction. Utility consumers in Illinois, for example, are able to join a consumer group that has saved them billions of dollars in electric bills. In conjunction with state government mailings and corporate billing envelopes, for instance, consumers receive a notice asking them to join a membership organization, controlled by dues-paying members, that advocates on consumers' behalf before utility regulatory bodies. This model, based on a simple solicitation insert in regular mailings that are sent out (and therefore add no postage costs), needs to be replicated around the country, and for many other industries—cable, banks, insurance, auto companies, and so on. There are many communication carriers for such notices that can be utilized under needed new state and federal laws.

These and other forms of independent consumer organization would not only redress specific consumer demands, they also would help create a consumer culture that places value on quality, good value, and ecological and social considerations in production processes. Banding together as consumers broadens horizons, creates countervailing political power to oligopolistic sellers, and their indentured government agencies, and contributes to a shift in the buyer paradigm from conspicuous to conscious and conscientious consumption, from an impoverished consumption to a better standard of living safeguarded by a just legal framework.

As with explanations of the new consumerism, so with strategies for its remedy: reasonable people can reasonably disagree on what is best. That something should be done, however, should be clear enough, especially after the important debate that follows. I applaud Julie Schor and her colleagues for initiating it.

EDITORS' PREFACE

JOSHUA COHEN AND JOEL ROGERS

We in the United States do lots of consuming. Moreover, the time we spend away from consuming is commonly devoted to doing more of it in the future: we work to make the money, think about what to buy, and shop for the stuff itself. Consumption, in short, is a national preoccupation, a way of life.

What accounts for this striking devotion? Is it a good or bad thing? And if it is bad, what sort of "politics of consumption" might remedy it.

In this New Democracy Forum, economist Juliet Schor proposes some answers to these questions. She traces our aspiration to increase consumption to our ideas about an acceptable standard of living—ideas we get by comparing our own position with the situations of others. Our desires are growing principally because we have been comparing ourselves with wealthier people, not only with the Joneses down the block, but also with the Joneses in 90210 (who have benefited handsomely from two decades of growing income inequality). Schor argues that increased private consumption is a bad thing, partly because we already consume so much, and partly because increasing private consumption is a self-defeating route to happiness: if doing well requires doing better than others, then lots of us are doomed to defeat. The right "politics of consumption" would, in turn, have to encourage people to downplay the importance of social comparisons in their ideas about an acceptable standard of living, and to encourage instead "consumption that is democratic, egalitarian, and available to all."

Schor's respondents disagree with her at nearly every turn, but the crux of the disagreement lies in the politics. Many respondents argue, or at least suggest, that a serious political movement can criticize the distribution of resources, but risks an unacceptable moralism if it makes a political issue of private consumption patterns themselves. Though the issue is not settled here, its ultimate resolution is central to our expectations of the economy, and will do much to define the character of democratic politics for the next generation.

1

THE NEW POLITICS OF CONSUMPTION

JULIET SCHOR

In contemporary American culture, consuming is as authentic as it gets. (Advertisements, getting a bargain, garage sales, and credit cards are firmly entrenched pillars of our way of life.) We shop on our lunch hours, patronize outlet malls on vacation, and satisfy our latest desires with a late-night click of a mouse.

Yet for all its popularity, the shopping mania provokes considerable dis-ease: many Americans worry about our preoccupation with getting and spending. They fear we are losing touch with more worthwhile values and ways of living. But the discomfort rarely goes much further than that; it never coheres into a persuasive, well-articulated critique of consumerism. By contrast, in the 1960s and early 1970s, a far-reaching critique of consumer culture was a part of our political discourse. Elements of the New Left, influenced by the Frankfurt school, as well as by John Kenneth Galbraith and others, put forward a scathing indictment. They argued that Americans had been manipulated into participating in a dumbed-down, artificial consumer culture, which yielded few true human satisfactions.

For reasons that are not hard to imagine, this particular approach was short-lived, even among critics of American society and culture. It seemed too patronizing to talk about manipulation or the "true needs" of average Americans. In its stead, critics adopted a more liberal point of view and deferred to individuals on consumer issues. Social critics again emphasized the distribution of resources, with the more economistic goal of maximizing the incomes of working people. The good life, they suggested, could be achieved by attaining a comfortable, middle-class standard of living. This outlook was particularly prevalent in economics, where even radical economists have long believed that income is the key to well-being. While radical political economy, as it came to be called, retained a powerful critique of alienation in production and the distribution of property, it abandoned the nascent intellectual project of analyzing the consumer sphere. Few economists now think about how we consume, and whether it reproduces class inequality, alienation, or power. "Stuff" is the part of the equation that the system is thought to have gotten nearly right.

Of course, many Americans retained a critical stance toward our consumer culture. They embody that stance in their daily lives, in the ways they live and raise their kids. The rejection of consumerism, if you will, has taken place principally at an individual level. It is not associated with a widely accepted intellectual analysis, and an associated critical politics of consumption.

But such a politics has become an urgent need. The average American now finds it harder to achieve a satisfying standard of living than did the average American twenty-five years ago. Work requires longer hours, jobs are less secure, and pressures to spend more intense. Consumption-induced environmental damage remains pervasive, and we are in the midst of widespread failures of public provision. While the current economic boom has allayed consumers' fears for the moment, many Americans have long-term worries about their ability to meet basic needs, ensure a decent standard of living for their children, and keep up with an ever-escalating consumption norm.

In response to these developments, social critics continue to focus on income. In his impressive analysis of the problems of contemporary American capitalism, *Fat and Mean*, economist David Gordon emphasizes income adequacy. The "vast majority of U.S. households," he argues, "can barely make ends meet. . . . Meager livelihoods are a typical condition, an average circumstance." Meanwhile, the Economic Policy Institute focuses on the distribution of income and wealth, arguing that the gains of the top 20 percent have jeopardized the well-being of the bottom 80 percent. Incomes have stagnated and the robust 3 percent growth rates of the 1950s and 1960s are long gone. If we have a consumption problem, this view implicitly states, we can solve it by getting more income into more people's hands. The goals are redistribution and growth.

It is difficult to take exception to this view. It combines a deep respect for individual choice (the liberal part) with a commitment to justice and equality (the egalitarian part). I held it myself for many years. But I now believe that by failing to look deeper, to examine the very nature of consumption, it has become too limiting. In short, I do not think that the "income solution" addresses some of the most profound failures of the current consumption regime.

Why not? First, consuming is part of the problem. Income (the solution) leads to consumption practices that exacerbate and reproduce class and social inequalities, resulting in, and perhaps even worsening, an unequal distribution of income. Second, the system is structured such that an adequate income is an elusive goal. That is because adequacy is relative, defined by reference to the incomes of others. Without an analysis of consumer desire and need, and a different framework for understanding what is adequate, we are likely to find ourselves, twenty years from now, arguing that a median income of $100,000—rather than half that—is adequate. These arguments underscore the social context of consumption: the ways in which our sense of social standing and belonging comes from what we consume. If true, they suggest that attempts to achieve equality or adequacy of individual incomes without changing consumption patterns will be self-defeating.

Finally, it is difficult to make an ethical argument that people in one of the world's richest countries need more when the global income gap is so wide, the disparity in world resource use so enormous, and the possibility that we are already consuming beyond Earth's ecological carrying capacity so likely. This third critique will get less attention in this essay—because it is more familiar, not because it is less important—but I will return to it in the conclusion.

I agree that justice requires a vastly more equal society, in terms of income and wealth. The question is whether we should also aim for a society in which our relationship to consuming changes, a society in which we consume differently. I argue here for such a perspective: for a critique of consumer culture and practices. Somebody needs to be for quality of life, not just quantity of stuff. And to be so requires an approach that does not trivialize consumption, but accords it the respect and centrality it deserves.

The New Consumerism

A new politics of consumption should begin with daily life, and with recent developments in the sphere of consumption. I describe these developments as "the new consumerism," by which I mean an upscaling of lifestyle norms; the pervasiveness of conspicuous, status goods and of competition for acquiring them; and the growing disconnection between consumer desires and incomes.

Social comparison and its dynamic manifestation—the need to "keep up"—have long been part of American culture. My term is *competitive consumption,* the idea that spending is in large part driven by a comparative or competitive process in which individuals try to keep up with the norms of the social group with which they identify, a "reference group." Although the term is new, the idea is not. Thorstein Veblen, James Duesenberry, Fred Hirsch, and Robert Frank have all written about the importance of relative position as a dominant spending motive. What's new is the redefinition of reference groups: today's comparisons are less likely to take place between or among households of similar means. Instead, the lifestyles of the upper middle class and the rich have become a more salient point of reference for people throughout the income distribution. Luxury, rather than mere comfort, is a widespread aspiration.

One reason for this shift to "upscale emulation" is the decline of the neighborhood as a focus of comparison. Economically speaking, neighborhoods are relatively homogeneous groupings. In the 1950s and 1960s, when Americans were keeping up with the Joneses down the street, they typically compared themselves with other households of similar incomes. Because of this focus on neighbors, the gap between aspirations and means tended to be moderate.

But as married women entered the workforce in larger numbers, particularly in white-collar jobs, they were exposed to a more economically diverse group of people, and became more likely to gaze upward. Neighborhood contacts correspondingly declined, and the workplace became a more prominent point of reference. Moreover, as people spent less time with neighbors and friends, and more time on the family-room couch, television became more important as a source of consumer cues and information. Because television shows are so heavily skewed to the "lifestyles of the rich and upper middle class," they inflate the viewer's perceptions of what others have, and by extension what is worth acquiring—what one must have in order to avoid being "out of it."

Trends in inequality also helped to create the new consumerism. Since the 1970s, the distribution of income and wealth have shifted decisively in the direction of the top 20 percent. The share of after-tax family income going to the top 20 percent rose from 41.4 percent in 1979 to 46.8 percent in 1996. The share of wealth controlled by the top 20 percent rose from 81.3 percent in 1983 to 84.3 percent in 1997. This windfall resulted in a surge in conspicuous spending at the top. Remember the 1980s—the decade of greed and excess? Beginning with the superrich, whose gains have been disproportionately higher, and trickling down to the merely affluent, visible status spending was the order of the day. Slowed down temporarily by the recession during the early 1990s, conspicuous luxury consumption has intensified during the current boom. Trophy homes, diamonds of a carat or more, granite countertops, and sport utility vehicles now are the primary consumer symbols. Television, as well as films, magazines, and newspapers, ensure that the remaining 80 percent of the nation is aware of the status purchasing that has swept the upper echelons.

In the meantime, upscale emulation had become well established. Researchers Susan Fournier and Michael Guiry found that 35 percent of their sample aspired to reach the top 6 percent of the income distribution, and another 49 percent aspired to the next 12 percent. Only 15 percent reported that they would be satisfied with "living a comfortable life," that is, being middle class. But 85 percent of the population cannot earn the six-figure incomes necessary to support upper-middle-class lifestyles. The result is a growing aspirational gap: with desires persistently outrunning incomes, many consumers find themselves frustrated. One survey of U.S. households found that the level of income needed to fulfill one's dreams doubled between 1986 and 1994, and is currently more than twice the median household income.

The rapid escalation of desire and need, relative to income, also may help to explain the precipitous decline in the savings rate, from roughly 8 percent in 1980, to 4 percent in the early 1990s, to the current level of zero. (The stock market boom may also be inducing households not to save; but financial assets are still highly concentrated, with half of all households at net worths of $10,000 or less, including the value of their homes.) About two thirds of American households do not save in a typical year. Credit card debt has skyrocketed, with unpaid balances now averaging about $7,000 per household and the typical household paying $1,000 each year in interest and penalties. These are not just low-income households. Bankruptcy rates continue to set new records, rising from 200,000 a year in 1980 to 1.4 million in 1998.

The new consumerism, with its growing aspirational gap, has begun to jeopardize the quality of American life. Within the middle class, and even the upper middle class, many families experience an almost threatening pressure to keep up, both for themselves and their children. They are deeply concerned about the rigors of the global economy, and the need to have their children attend "good" schools. This means living in a community with relatively high housing costs. For some households this also means providing their children with advantages purchased on the private market (computers, lessons, extracurriculars, private schooling). Keeping two adults in the labor market—as so many families do, to earn the incomes to stay middle class —is expensive, not only because of the second car, child care costs, and career wardrobe. It also creates the need for timesaving, but costly, commodities and services, such as take-out food and dry cleaning, as well as stress-relieving activities. Finally, the financial tightrope that so many households walk—high expenses, low savings—is a constant source of stress and worry. While precise estimates are difficult to come by, one can argue that somewhere between a quarter and a half of all households live paycheck to paycheck.

These problems are magnified for low-income households. Their sources of income have become increasingly erratic and inadequate on account of employment instability, the proliferation of part-time jobs, and restrictions on welfare payments. Yet most low-income households remain firmly integrated within consumerism. They are targets for credit card companies, who find them an easy mark. They watch more television, and are more exposed to its desire-creating influences. Low-income children are more likely to be exposed to commercials at school, as well as home. The growing prominence of the values of the market, materialism, and economic success make financial failure more consequential and painful.

These are the effects at the household level. The new consumerism has also set in motion another dynamic: it siphons off resources that could be used for alternatives to private consumption. We use our income in four basic ways: private consumption, public consumption, private savings, and leisure. When consumption standards can be met easily out of current income, there is greater willingness to support public goods, save privately, and cut back on time spent at work (in other words, to "buy leisure"). Conversely, when lifestyle norms are upscaled more rapidly than income is, private consumption "crowds out" alternative uses of income. That is arguably what happened in the 1980s and 1990s: resources shifting into private consumption, and away from free time, the public sector, and saving. Hours of work have risen dramatically, saving rates have plummeted, public funds for education, recreation, and the arts have fallen in the wake of a

grass-roots tax revolt. The timing suggests a strong coinci-
dence between these developments and the intensification
of competitive consumption, though I would have to do
more systematic research before arguing causality. Indeed,
this scenario makes good sense of an otherwise surprising
finding: that indicators of "social health" or "genuine progress" (that is, basic quality-of-life measures) began to di-
verge from GDP in the mid-1970s, after moving in tandem
for decades. Can it be that consuming and prospering are no
longer compatible states?

To be sure, other social critics have noted some of these
trends. And they often draw radically different conclusions.
For example, there is now a conservative jeremiad that
points to the recent tremendous increases in consumption
and concludes that Americans just don't realize how good
they have it, that they have become overly entitled and
spoiled. Reduced expectations, they say, will cure our dis-
contents. A second, related perspective suggests that the solution lies in an act of psychological independence—individuals can just ignore the upward shift in consumption
norms, remaining perfectly content to descend in the social
hierarchy.

These perspectives miss the essence of consumption dy-
namics. Americans did not suddenly become greedy. The
aspirational gap has been created by structural changes,
such as the decline of community and social connection, the
intensification of inequality, the growing role of mass media, and heightened penalties for failing in the labor market.

Upscaling is mainly defensive, and has both psychological and practical dimensions.

Similarly, the profoundly social nature of consumption ensures that these issues cannot be resolved by pure acts of will. Our notions of what is adequate, necessary, or luxurious are shaped by the larger social context. Most of us are deeply tied into our particular class and other group identities, and our spending patterns help reproduce them.

Thus, a collective, not just an individual, response is necessary. Someone needs to address the larger question of the consumer culture itself. But doing so risks incurring complaints about being intrusive, patronizing, or elitist. We need to understand better the ideas that fuel those complaints.

Consumer Knows Best

The current consumer boom rests on growth in incomes, wealth, and credit. But it also rests on something more intangible: social attitudes toward consumer decision making and choices. Ours is an ideology of noninterference—the view that one should be able to buy what one likes, where one likes, and as much as one likes, with nary a glance from the government, neighbors, ministers, or political parties. Consumption is perhaps the clearest example of an individual behavior that our society takes to be almost wholly personal, completely outside the purview of social concern and policy. The consumer is king. And queen.

This view has much to recommend it. After all, who would relish the idea of sumptuary legislation, rationing, or government controls on what can be produced or purchased? The liberal approach to consumption combines a deep respect for the consumer's ability to act in his or her own best interest and an emphasis on the efficiency gains of unregulated consumer markets: a commitment to liberty and the general welfare.

Cogent as it is, however, this view is vulnerable on a number of grounds. Structural biases and market failures in the operation of consumer markets undermine its general validity; consumer markets are neither so free nor so efficient as the conventional story suggests. The basis of a new consumer policy should be an understanding of the presence of structural distortions in consumers' choices, the importance of social inequalities and power in consumption practices, a more sophisticated understanding of consumer motivations, and serious analysis of the processes that form our preferences. To appreciate the force of these criticisms, we need a sharper statement of the position they reject.

The Conventional View

The liberal view on markets for consumer goods has adherents in many disciplines, but its core analytic argument comes from standard economic theory, which begins from some well-known assumptions about consumers and the markets in which they operate.

1. Consumers are rational. They act to maximize their own well-being. They know what they prefer, and make decisions accordingly. Their "preferences" are taken as given, as relatively unchanging, and as unproblematic in a normative sense. They do not act capriciously, impulsively, or self-destructively.

2. Consumers are well informed. They have perfect information about the products offered in the market. They know about all relevant (to the consumer) characteristics pertaining to the production and use of the product.

3. Consumer preferences are consistent (both at a point in time and over time). Consistency at a point in time means transitivity: If A is preferred to B and B to C, then A will be preferred to C. (In other words, if roast beef is preferred to hamburgers and hamburgers to hot dogs, then roast beef is preferred to hot dogs.) Consistency over time can be thought of as a "no regrets" assumption. If the consumer is faced with a choice of a product that yields satisfaction in the present but has adverse consequences in the future—eat chocolate today and feel great, but be five unwanted pounds heavier by next week—and the consumer chooses that product today, he or she will not regret the choice when the future arrives. (This does not mean the extra pounds are welcomed, only that the pleasure of the chocolate continues to outweigh the pain of the pounds.)

4. Each consumer's preferences are independent of other consumers' preferences. We are self-contained in a social sense. If I want a sport utility vehicle, it is because I like it, not because my neighbor does. The trendiness of a product does not affect my desire to have it, either positively or negatively.

5. *The production and consumption of goods have no "external" effects.* There are no consequences for the welfare of others that are unreflected in product prices. (A well-known example of external effects is pollution, which imposes costs on others that are not reflected in the price of the good that produces the pollution.)

6. *There are complete and competitive markets in alternatives to consumption.* Alternatives to consumption include savings, public goods, and the "purchase" of leisure. Unless these alternatives are available, the choice of consumption, over other uses of economic resources, may not be the optimal outcome.

Taken together, and combined with conditions of free entry and exit of firms providing consumer goods, these assumptions imply that no consumer policy is the best consumer policy. Individual consumers know best and will act in their own interest. Firms will provide what the consumers want; those that don't will not survive a competitive marketplace. Competition and rationality together ensure that consumers will be sovereign, that is, that their interests will "rule." And the results will be better than any we could achieve through government regulation or political action.

To be sure, conventional theory and policy have always admitted some deviations from these highly idealized conditions. In some areas interventionist policy has been long-standing. First, some consumers are not considered to be fully rational, for example, children and, in an earlier era, women. Because kids are not thought to be capable of acting in their own interest, the state justifies protective policies, such as the restriction of advertising aimed at them. Second, the state has traditionally regulated highly addictive or harmful commodities, such as drugs, alcohol, and explosives. (As the debates surrounding the legalization of drugs make clear, the analytical basis for this policy is by no means universally accepted.) A third class of highly regulated commodities involves the trappings of sex: pornography, contraceptives, sexual paraphernalia, and so forth. Here the rationale is more puritanical. American society has always been uncomfortable about sex and willing to override its bias against consumer regulation because of that. Finally, the government has for much of this century, though less forcefully since the Reagan administration, attempted to ensure minimum standards of product safety and quality.

These exceptions aside, the standard model holds strongly to the idea that unfettered markets yield the optimal outcomes, a conclusion that follows logically and inexorably from the initial assumptions. Obviously, the assumptions of the standard model are extreme, and the real world deviates from them. On that everyone agrees. The question is by how much, how often, and under what conditions? Is the world sufficiently different from this model that its conclusions are misguided?

Serious empirical investigations suggest that these assumptions do not adequately describe a wide range of consumer behaviors. The simple rational-economic model is reasonable for predicting some fraction of choice behavior for some class of goods—apples versus oranges, milk versus orange juice—but it is inadequate when we are led to more consequential issues: consumption versus leisure, products with high symbolic content, fashion, consumer credit, and so on. In particular, it exaggerates how rational, informed, and consistent people are. It overstates their independence. And it fails to address the pressures that consumerism imposes on individuals with respect to available choices and the consequences of various consumption decisions. Understand those pressures, and you may well arrive at very different conclusions about politics and policy.

RATIONAL, DELIBERATIVE, AND IN CONTROL?

The economic model presents the typical consumer as deliberative and highly forward-looking, not subject to impulsive behavior. Shopping is seen as an information-gathering exercise in which the buyer looks for the best possible deal for a product he or she has decided to purchase. Consumption choices represent optimizing within an environment of deliberation, control, and long-term planning.

Were such a picture accurate it would be news (and news of a very bad sort) to a whole industry of advertisers, marketers, and consultants whose research on consumer behavior tells a very different story. Indeed, their findings are difficult to reconcile with the picture of the consumer as highly deliberative and purposive.

Consider some of the stylized facts of modern marketing. For example, there is the "law of the invariant right": shoppers overwhelmingly turn right, rather than left, upon entering a store. This is consistent with the rational search model only if products are disproportionately to be found on the right side of the aisle. Or consider the fact that products placed in the so-called *decompression zone* at the entrance to a store are 30 percent less likely to be purchased than those placed beyond it. Or that the number of feet into a store the customer walks is correlated with the number of items purchased. It's far harder to square these findings with "rational" behavior than with an unplanned and contingent action. Finally, the standard model has a very hard time explaining the fact that if while shopping a woman is accidentally brushed from behind, her propensity to purchase falls precipitously.

Credit cards present another set of anomalies for the reigning assumptions. Surveys suggest that most people who acquire credit cards say that they do not intend to borrow on them; yet roughly two thirds do. The use of credit cards leads to higher expenditures. Psychological research suggests that even the visual cue of a credit card logo spurs spending. Survey data show that many people are in denial about the level of credit card debt that they have, on average underestimating by a factor of two. And the explosion of personal bankruptcies, now running at roughly 1.5 million a year, can be taken as evidence of a lack of foresight, planning, and control for at least some consumers.

More generally, credit card habits are one example of what economists call "hyperbolic discounting," that is, an extreme tendency to discount the future. Such a perspective calls into question the idea of time consistency—the ability of individuals to plan spending optimally throughout their lifetimes, to save enough for the future, or to delay gratification. If people are constitutionally inclined to be hyperbolic discounters, as some are now arguing, then forced-saving programs such as Social Security and government-sponsored retirement accounts, restriction on access to credit, waiting periods for major purchases, and a variety of other approaches might improve well-being. Compulsive buying, as well as the milder and far more pervasive control problems that many consumers manifest, can also be incorporated into this framework.

The model of deliberative and informed rationality is also ill adapted to account for the phenomenon of brand preference, perhaps the backbone of the modern consumer market. As any beginning student of advertising knows, much of what advertising does is take functionally identical or similar goods and differentiate them on the basis of a variety of nonoperational traits. The consumer is urged to buy Pepsi because it represents the future, or Reebok shoes because the company stands for strong women. The consumer develops a brand preference, and believes that his or her brand is superior in quality. The difficulty for the standard model arises because without labels consumers are often unable to distinguish among brands, or fail to choose their favorites. From the famous beer taste test of the 1960s (brand loyalists misidentified their beers), to cosmetics, garments, and other tests of more recent vintage, it seems that we love our brands, but we often can't tell which brands are which.

What can we conclude from consumers' inability to tell one washing powder, lipstick, sweater, or toothpaste from another? Not necessarily that they are foolishly paying a brand premium for goods. (Although there are some consumers who do fall into this category; they wouldn't pay the brand premium, as distinct from a true quality premium, if they knew it existed.) What is more generally true, I believe, is that many consumers do not understand why they prefer one brand over another, or desire particular products. This is because there is a significant dimension of consumer desire that operates at the nonrational level. Consumers believe their brand loyalties are driven by functional dimensions, but a whole host of other motivators are at work, for example, social meanings as constructed by advertisers; personal fantasies projected on to goods; competitive pressures. While this behavior is not properly termed *irrational,* it is not conscious, deliberative, and narrowly purposive. Consumers are not deluded, duped, or completely manipulated. But neither do they act like profit-maximizing entrepreneurs or scientific management experts. The realm of consumption, as a rich historical literature has taught us, has long been a "dream world," where fantasy, play, inner desire, escape, and emotion loom large. This is a significant part of what draws us to it.

CONSUMPTION IS SOCIAL

Within economics, the major alternative to the assumption that individuals' preferences are independent—that people do not want things because others want them—is the "relative" income, positional, or "competitive consumption" perspective noted on page 8. In this model, a person's well-being depends on his or her relative consumption—how it compares to some selected group of others. Such positioning is one of the hallmarks of the new consumerism.

Of course, social comparison predates the 1980s. In 1984, French sociologist Pierre Bourdieu explored the social patterning of consumption and taste in *Distinction: A Social Critique of the Judgment of Taste.* Bourdieu found that family socialization processes and educational experiences are the primary determinants of taste for a wide range of cultural goods, including food, dress, and home decor. In contrast to the liberal approach, in which consumption choices are both personal and trivialized, that is, socially inconsequential, Bourdieu argues that class status is gained, lost, and reproduced in part through everyday acts of consumer behavior. Being dressed incorrectly or displaying "vulgar" manners can cost a person a management or professional job. Conversely, one can gain entry into social circles, or build lucrative business contacts, by revealing appropriate tastes, manners, and culture. Thus, consumption practices become important in maintaining the basic structures of power and inequality that characterize our world. Such a perspective helps to illuminate why we invest so much meaning in consumer goods—for the middle class its very existence is at stake. And it suggests that people who care about inequality should talk explicitly about the stratification of consumption practices.

If we accept that what we buy is deeply implicated in the structures of social inequality, then the idea that unregulated consumption promotes the general welfare collapses. When people care only about relative position, then general increases in income and consumption do not yield gains in well-being. If my ultimate consumer goal is to maintain parity with my sister, or my neighbor, or Frasier, and our consumption moves in tandem, my well-being is not improved. I am on a "positional treadmill." Indeed, because consuming has costs (in terms of time, effort, and natural resources), positional treadmills can have serious negative effects on well-being. The "working harder to stay in place" mantra of the early 1990s expresses some of this sentiment. In a pure reversal of the standard prescription, collective interventions that stabilize norms through government policy or other mechanisms raise rather than lower welfare. People should welcome initiatives that reduce the pressure to keep up with a rising standard.

Free and Structurally Unbiased?

The dynamic of positionally driven spending suggests that Americans are "overconsuming" at least those private goods that figure in our consumption comparisons. There is another reason we may be overconsuming, which has to do with the problems in markets for alternatives to status or positional goods. In particular, I am referring to nonpositional private consumption, household savings, public goods, and leisure. Generally speaking, if the markets for these alternatives are incomplete or noncompetitive, or do not fully account for social benefits and costs, then overconsumption with respect to private consumption may result. I do not believe this is the case with household savings: financial markets are highly competitive and offer households a wide range of ways to save. (The deceptive and aggressive tactics of consumer credit companies might be reckoned a distortion in this market, but I'll leave that aside.) Similarly, I do not argue that the markets for private consumer goods that we tend not to compete about are terribly flawed. Still, there are two markets in which the standard assumptions do not apply: the market for public goods and the market for time. Here I believe the deviations from the assumptions are large, and extremely significant.

In the case of public goods there are at least two big problems. The first is the underproduction of a clean environment. Because environmental damage is typically not included in the price of the product which causes it (for example, cars, toxic chemicals, pesticides), we overconsume environmentally damaging commodities. Indeed, because all production has an impact on the environment, we overconsume virtually all commodities. This means that we consume too much in toto, in comparison to nonenvironmentally damaging human activities.

The second problem arises from the fact that business interests—the interests of the producers of private goods—have privileged access to the government and disproportionately influence policy. Because they are typically opposed to public provision, the "market" for public goods is structurally biased against provision. In comparison to what a truly democratic state might provide, we find that a business-dominated government skews outcomes in the direction of private production. We don't get enough, or good enough, education, arts, recreation, mass transport, and other conventional public goods. We get too many cars, too many clothes, too many collectibles.

For those public goods that are complementary with private spending (roads and cars versus bicycle lanes and bicycles) this bias constrains the choices available to individuals. Without the bicycle lanes or mass transport, private cars are unavoidable. Because so much of our consumption is linked to larger collective decisions, the individual consumer is always operating under particular constraints. Once we move to HDTV, our current televisions will become obsolete. As public telephone booths disappear, mobile phones become more necessary. Without adequate public libraries, we need to purchase more books.

We also underproduce "leisure." That's because employers make it difficult to choose free time, rather than long hours and higher incomes. To use the economist's jargon, the labor market offerings are incomplete with respect to trade-offs of time and money. Employers can exact severe penalties when individuals want to work part-time or forgo raises in favor of more vacations or days off. In some jobs the options are just not available; in others the sacrifices in terms of career mobility and benefits are disproportionate to any productivity costs to the employer.

This is not a minor point. The standard model assumes that employees are free to vary their hours, and that whatever combination of hours and income results represents the preferences of employees. But if employees lack the opportunity to vary their working hours, or to use improvements in productivity to reduce their work time, then we can in no way assume that the trajectory of consumption reflects people's preferences. There may well be a path for the economy that involves less work and less stuff, and is preferred by people to the high-work/high-consumption track. But if that option is blocked, then the fact that we buy a lot can no longer be taken ipso facto as proof of our inherent consumer desires. We may merely be doing what is on offer. Because free time is now a strongly desired alternative to income for large numbers of employees, this argument is more than a theoretical possibility. It has become one of the most pressing failures of the current moment.

A Politics of Consumption

The idea that consumption is private should not, then, be a conversation stopper. But what should a politics of consumption look like? To start the discussion, not to provide final answers, I suggest seven basic elements:

1. A right to a decent standard of living. This familiar idea is especially important now because it points us to a fundamental distinction between what people need and what they want. In the not very distant past, this dichotomy was not only well understood, but the basis of data collection and social policy. Need was a social concept with real force. All that's left now is an economy of desire. This is reflected in polling data. Just over 40 percent of adults earning $50,000 to $100,000 a year, and 27 percent of those earning more than $100,000, agree that "I cannot afford to buy everything I really need." One third and 19 percent, respectively, agree that "I spend nearly all of my money on the basic necessities of life." I believe that our politics would profit from reviving a discourse of need, in which we talk about the material requirements for every person and household to participate fully in society. Of course, there are many ways in which such a right might be enforced: government income transfers or vouchers, direct provision of basic needs, employment guarantees, and the like. For reasons of space, I leave that discussion aside; the main point is to revive the distinction between needs and desires.

2. *Quality of life rather than quantity of stuff.* Twenty-five years ago quality-of-life indicators began moving in an opposite direction from our measures of income, or Gross Domestic Product, a striking divergence from historic trends. Moreover, the accumulating evidence on well-being, at least its subjective measures (and to some extent objective measures, such as health), suggests that above the poverty line, income is relatively unimportant in affecting well-being. This may be because what people care about is relative, not absolute, income. Or it may be because increases in output undermine precisely those factors that do yield welfare. Here I have in mind the growing work time requirements of the market economy, and the concomitant decline in family, leisure, and community time; the adverse impacts of growth on the natural environment; and the potential link between growth and social capital.

This argument that consumption is not the same as well-being has great potential to resonate with millions of Americans. Large majorities hold ambivalent views about consumerism. They struggle with ongoing conflicts between materialism and an alternative set of values stressing family, religion, community, social commitment, equity, and personal meaning. We should be articulating an alternative vision of a quality of life, rather than a quantity of stuff. That is a basis on which to argue for a restructuring of the labor market to allow people to choose for time, or to penalize companies that require excessive hours for employees. It is also a basis for creating alternative indicators to the GNP, positive policies to encourage civic engagement, support for parents, and so forth.

3. Ecologically sustainable consumption. Current consumption patterns are wreaking havoc on the planetary ecology. Global warming is perhaps the best known, but many other consumption habits have major environmental impacts. Sport utility vehicles, air-conditioning, and foreign travel are all energy-intensive, and contribute to global warming. Larger homes use more energy and building resources, destroy open space, and increase the use of toxic chemicals. All those granite countertops being installed in American kitchens were carved out of mountains around the world, leaving in their wake a blighted landscape. Our daily newspaper with our morning coffee is contributing to deforestation and loss of species diversity. Something as simple as a T-shirt plays its part, since cotton cultivation accounts for a significant fraction of world pesticide use. Consumers know far less about the environmental impacts of their daily consumption habits than they should. And while the solution lies in greater part with corporate and governmental practices, people who are concerned about equality should be joining forces with environmentalists who are trying to educate, mobilize, and change practices at the neighborhood and household level.

4. Democratization of consumption practices. One of the

central arguments I have made is that consumption practices reflect and perpetuate structures of inequality and power. This is particularly true in the "new consumerism," with its emphasis on luxury, expensiveness, exclusivity, rarity, uniqueness, and distinction. These are the values that consumer markets are plying, to the middle and lower-middle classes. (That is what Martha Stewart is doing at Kmart.)

But who needs to accept these values? Why not stand for consumption that is democratic, egalitarian, and available to all? How about making "access," rather than exclusivity, cool, by exposing the industries such as fashion, home decor, or tourism, which are pushing the upscaling of desire? This point speaks to the need for both cultural change, as well as policies that might facilitate it. Why not tax high-end "status" versions of products while allowing the low-end models to be sold tax free?

5. A politics of retailing and the "cultural environment." The new consumerism has been associated with the homogenization of retail environments and a pervasive shift toward the commercialization of culture. The same megastores can be found everywhere, creating a blandness in the cultural environment. Advertising and marketing are also pervading hitherto relatively protected spaces, such as schools, doctors' offices, media programming (rather than commercial time), and so on. In my local mall, the main restaurant offers a booklike menu comprising advertisements for unrelated products. The daily paper looks more like a consumer's guide to food, wine, computer electronics, and tourism and less like a purveyor of news. We should be talking about these issues, and the ways in which corporations are remaking our public institutions and space. Do we value diversity in retailing? Do we want to preserve small retail outlets? How about ad-free zones? Commercial-free public education? Here too public policy can play a role by outlawing certain advertising in certain places and institutions, by financing publicly controlled media, and enacting zoning regulations that take diversity as a positive value.

6. An exposé of commodity "fetishism." Everything we consume has been produced. So a new politics of consumption must take into account the labor, environmental, and other conditions under which products are made, and argue for high standards. This argument has been of great political importance in recent years, with public exposure of the so-called global sweatshop in the apparel, footwear, and fashion industries. Companies fear for their public images, and consumers appear willing to pay a little more for products when they know they have been produced responsibly. There are fruitful and essential linkages between production, consumption, and the environment that we should be making.

7. A consumer movement and governmental policy. Much of what I have been arguing for could occur as a result of a consumer movement. Indeed, the revitalization of the labor movement calls out for an analogous revitalization of long-dormant consumers. We need independent organizations of consumers to pressure companies, influence the political agenda, provide objective product information, and articulate a vision of an appealing and humane consumer sphere. We also need a consumer movement to pressure the state to enact the kinds of policies that the foregoing analysis suggests are needed. These include taxes on luxury and status consumption, green taxes and subsidies, new policies toward advertising, more sophisticated regulations on consumer credit, international labor and environmental standards, revamping of zoning regulations to favor retail diversity, and the preservation of open space. There is a vast consumer policy agenda that has been mainly off the table. It's time to put it back on.

2

MARKET FAILURES

ROBERT H. FRANK

Is Juliet Schor right that American spending patterns have gone astray? At a quick glance, it would certainly appear so. Despite growing threats from *E. coli, listeria,* and other deadly organisms, we cite financial distress to explain why we've cut FDA inspections of meat-processing plants by more than 75 percent in the last decade, even as we've continued to build larger houses and buy heavier sport utility vehicles. And each year we postpone repairs on structurally unsound bridges and shut down cost-effective drug-treatment programs, even as our spending on luxury goods continues to grow four times as quickly as spending overall.

Behavioral science now provides additional grounds to question the wisdom of our current spending patterns. Scores of careful studies show that we would be happier and healthier if we spent less on luxury goods, saved more, and provided more support for basic public services.

But this raises an obvious question: if we'd be better off if we spent our money differently, why don't we? In her essay (and in her recent book, *The Overspent American*), Juliet Schor surveys a variety of possible explanations. Communitarians cite a decline in social capital, noting that affluent Americans sequestered in gated communities are increasingly insulated from the consequences of our neglected public sphere. Social theorists emphasize the imperatives of class and identity, which drive many to proclaim their superiority over others through the purchase of costly goods. Other critics stress the influence of sophisticated marketing campaigns, which kindle demands for things we don't really need. Professor Schor especially favors this marketing explanation, and she argues forcefully on its behalf, as did John Kenneth Galbraith more than forty years ago in *The Affluent Society.*

Despite its distinguished pedigree, however, the marketing explanation also has a drawback: although it can account for a bias toward luxury-consumption spending, it does not seem to explain why things have gotten so much worse. Television advertising has been with us since the early 1950s, after all, and salesmanship in various other forms since before the dawn of the industrial age.

Why, then, are the apparent distortions so much larger today? In my recent book, *Luxury Fever,* I suggest that one reason may lie in a simple change in the economic incentives we face. This change is rooted in a fundamental shift in the distributions of income and wealth in America that began in the early 1970s.

Whereas incomes grew at about 3 percent a year for families up and down the income ladder between 1945 and 1973, most earnings growth since 1973 has gone to families at the top. For example, the top 1 percent of earners have captured more than 70 percent of all earnings growth during the last two decades, a time during which median real-family income has been stagnant and the incomes of the bottom fifth have declined about 10 percent. Reinforcing these changes has been a parallel shift in the distribution of wealth, much of it driven by the spectacular run-up in stock prices.

Increasing inequality has caused real, unavoidable harm to families in the middle class—even to those who now earn a little more than they used to—by making it more difficult to achieve balance in their personal spending decisions. The problem stems from the fact that the things we need so often depend on what others have. As Nobel laureate Amartya Sen has pointed out, a middle-class Indian living in a remote mountain village has no need for a car, but a middle-class resident of Los Angeles cannot meet even the most minimal demands of social existence without one.

When those at the top spend more on interview suits, others just below them must spend more as well, or else face lower odds of being hired. When upper-middle-class professionals buy six-thousand-pound Range Rovers, others with lower incomes must buy heavier vehicles as well, or else face greater risks of dying. Residents in a community in which the custom is to host dinners for twelve need bigger dining rooms than if the custom were dinners for eight.

So when top earners build larger houses—a perfectly normal response to their sharply higher incomes—others just below them will have greater need to spend more as well, and so on all the way down. Because of the growing income gap, the size of the average American house built in 1999 was roughly twenty-two hundred square feet, up from fifteen hundred square feet in 1970.

The middle-income family that buys this house must carry a significantly larger mortgage than the buyer of the average house carried in 1970. And because public school quality is closely linked to local real estate taxes, which in turn are closely linked to average house prices within each school district, families must buy an average-priced house or else send their children to below-average schools. So even the middle-income family that doesn't want a bigger house may feel it really has no choice but to buy one.

Yet because this family has no more real income than it had in 1970, it must now carry more debt and work longer hours than before. Little wonder, then, that despite the longest economic expansion on record, with the unemployment rate at a twenty-nine-year low, one American family in sixty-eight filed for bankruptcy last year, almost seven times the rate in 1980. Our national savings rate is now negative, which means that we are currently spending more each month than we earn.

My claim, in a nutshell, is that the imbalance in our current spending patterns may be viewed as a market failure caused by consumption externalities: by the fact that greater consumption by some people imposes costs on others. An important strategic advantage of this explanation is that it is grounded in the very same theoretical framework that animates the beliefs of the most ardent defenders of the status quo. Thus, as even conservative economists have long recognized, when one family's spending decisions impose negative consequences on others, Adam Smith's invisible hand simply cannot be expected to produce the best overall spending pattern.

The good news is that if consumption externalities are what lead us to work too hard, spend too much, and save too little, a relatively simple legislative fix is at hand. Just as we have persuaded legislators that effluent taxes and other economic incentives are better than regulation as a way to curb pollution and other environmental externalities, so too might we eventually persuade them that it is better to curb consumption externalities through the tax system than by trying to micromanage personal spending decisions.

In *Luxury Fever*, I suggest that we scrap our current progressive tax on income in favor of a far more steeply progressive tax on consumption. Because total consumption for each family can be measured as the simple difference between the amount it earns each year (as currently reported to the IRS) and the amount it saves, such a tax would be relatively easy to administer. And if the tax were coupled with a large standard deduction (say, $7,500 per person) and had low marginal tax rates on low levels of consumption, it would be even less burdensome for the poor than our current income tax.

More important, it would provide top earners with strong incentives to save more and limit the rate at which they increase the size of their mansions. Their doing so would reinforce the incentives on those just below the top to do likewise, and so on all the way down. Phased in gradually, this tax would slowly reduce the share of national income devoted to consumption and increase the corresponding share devoted to investment. Total spending would continue at levels sufficient to maintain full employment, and greater investment would lead to more rapid growth in productivity.

The tax could be set up so that the revenue raised from each income class would be roughly the same as comes from each under the current system. But persuasive evidence suggests that if legislators were to set rates on top spenders high enough to raise greater revenue than under the current system, both rich and poor would benefit significantly. Since beyond some point it is relative, not absolute, consumption that matters, top earners would not really suffer if the tax led all of them to increase the sizes of their mansions at a slower rate. Yet they and others would reap large benefits from the restoration of long-neglected public services.

Persuading legislators to enact a steeply progressive consumption tax will not be easy. Its congressional sponsors could count on being pilloried by opponents as tax-and-spend liberals. Yet the progressive consumption tax is hardly a fringe idea. A bill proposing a tax with essentially the same features (the "Unlimited Savings Allowance Tax," or USA Tax) was introduced in the U.S. Senate in 1995 by Pete Domenici (R-N.M.) and Sam Nunn (D-Ga.).

By suggesting that our current consumption imbalance is a result, in large measure, of consumption externalities, I do not mean that other explanations for the imbalance are wrong. Social capital has declined. Class also matters, and there is no denying the influence of commercial advertising.

If a political solution is what we seek, however, there may be considerable strategic advantage in focusing on externalities. It is difficult to imagine Congress approving legislation aimed at transforming class consciousness or eliminating commercial advertising. But we have a long tradition of collective action to control externalities—of discouraging some people from imposing uncompensated costs on others. And as Madison Avenue hucksters have known all along, it is a lot easier to sell with the grain than against it.

THE STONE AGE

JAMES B. TWITCHELL

Trophy homes, diamonds of a carat or more, granite countertops, and sport utility vehicles are the primary consumer symbols of the late 1990s.

—Juliet Schor

Oh my God. Things are worse than I had thought. Sure, I knew there were too many Gucci handbags around. And I knew that as I drove my gorgeous two-ton Volvo to work I was seeing entirely too many of those ugly six-thousand-pound SUVs on road. Ditto those too-big diamonds and trophy homes. But before reading Professor Schor's essay, I did not know about all those granite countertops. Where the hell did they come from?

What students of Ivy League economists soon realize is that, just as shoppers on Rodeo Drive have "home brands" around which they concoct a consumption constellation, so too do academic Eeyores have their own *objets fixes*. John Kenneth Galbraith had his Cadillac tail fins, Robert Frank has his Patek Philippe wristwatch, and now Juliet Schor adds the granite countertop. Veblen made first claim on the trophy house.

Look, how come it's okay to lay a slab of granite four

times the size of a countertop over the body of dead Uncle Louie, carve a few dates in it, and then leave it alone for years, while it's a sign of a really urgent problem—the dreaded "luxury fever"—when the slab appears in the kitchen where it can actually be used and—gasp!—enjoyed?

I realize that to focus on these two words, *granite countertop,* may be to willfully neglect the Big Points of Schor's essay. What about all the other stuff: debt, status anxiety, mass media manipulation, and simple fair play for those poorer than we are? I focus on the minute particulars because it's on specific items of consumption that the "we must control it" argument rests. Or so it seems to me.

You see, from my point of view, what these academic economists have trouble with is not consumption but taste. Buy a rare edition of John Milton's *Comus* for $400,000 (which, thanks to Xerox, has almost no scholarly value) and you won't hear a peep from the lefties over in the econ department. But buy a videocassette of *Debbie Does Dallas* for four dollars, show it to them on your big-screen TV in your entertainment center with the Bose wraparound speakers, and all hell breaks loose.

Don't even think about doing this if you are poor. The consumption police will be at your door. The first word they will use is *waste.* Then they'll say you can't afford it. You're already maxed out. But coming next is the most interesting word, and it should always ring a bell. The word is *luxury.* When you hear them use this word, grab your credit cards and head for the hills.

Luxury is a word like *predator* or *weed*. There is no such thing in nature as a predator or a weed. You hear the words, however, just before someone reaches for a gun or a spade. Mark my words, the next word you hear after luxury is . . . *tax*.

We are not the first generation to encounter this. It started with the Greeks, then the Christians had a go at it. But if you really want to see it played out splendidly, go read the raging battle in the eighteenth century, with Adam Smith and Bernard Mandeville on one free-market side, and Tobias Smollett and Henry Fielding on the "we have an urgent problem here" side. Or if reading is not your style— thanks to the evil ways of that nasty Mr. Television, who has filled us with insatiable desire—you can tune in to the show by looking at Hogarth's engravings. Start with the disputed *Taste in High Life* and work your way to *A Harlot's Progress, A Rake's Progress,* and finish up with *Marriage à la Mode.* Little wonder sumptuary taxes continued up through the Industrial Revolution and still appear in bits and pieces.

So what's to be done about our "urgent" problem? Not much. Try to tax and shame it into behaving properly if you want, but history shows it won't work. The market keeps humming along, occasionally breaking down, and then rebuilding itself. Fear and greed do their thing. Downshifters will downshift, upshifters will upshift. Then they'll reverse gears and do it all over again. Shirtsleeves to shirtsleeves. Like it or not, the market will do a pretty fair job of inflicting the penalties of living too long in the lap of luxury.

But more to the point, what can be done about those Ivy League economists and their "new politics of consumption"?

Here's my take-two-aspirin-and-see-me-in-the-morning prescription. Professor Schor should

1. Rent Steve Martin's *The Jerk* (1979)
2. Read Anthony Trollope's *The Way We Live Now* (1875)

She'll learn from watching *The Jerk* that even jerks know that we don't buy things, we buy meanings. Consider that if we drink the advertising, not the beer, maybe it's the advertising we're after. More often than not what we once condemned as luxury has become necessity for a reason—it's good stuff, even though granite countertops may cause a temporary problem along the way. And she'll learn from Trollope that a world in which social status is based on bloodline, church pew, and the name of your club is not so hot—especially if you're Melmotte, the newcomer, a Jew. And this is nothing compared to how much mobility you'll get if you are a woman, a black, an entrepreneur, or just a working stiff. Consumerism is not pretty, but it beats the alternatives put forward so far.

So far I've focused on the minute particulars: the granite countertop and all that I think it represents about "inappropriate" consumer taste and "appropriate" economic judgment. Let me end metaphysically, like the poet Shelley, "pinnacled dim in the intense inane."

To me the problem is not that we are too materialistic, but

that we are not materialistic enough. If we knew what goods meant we wouldn't be so susceptible to, so needful of, the addition of meaning. Marketing wouldn't work. Madison Avenue would close down.

But instead we know stuff is important. We love having things. Exchanging things. Hording things. Stealing things. Even economists call them "goods and services." Of course we fetishize objects. How the hell do you think they get meaning? That meaning is so important that we willingly go into debt to get it. Especially when we are young.

Although modern consumption may share a few characteristics with Victorian consumption (that is, tuberculosis), it is not a disease to be controlled by Drs. Tax and Shame. It is a response to life as we are living it. When you think about consumption from this point of view, you realize that it is not objects, even luxury objects, that are the problem. It is the meaning of life that has become perplexing in a world bereft of bloodlines, family pews, social clubs, and the like. Face it: you are what you consume, not what you make. You are the logo on your T-shirt, not a descendant of a Mayflower passenger.

What we lack is not a politics of consumption so much as a religion of consumption. Not to sound too eerie, but the development of that religion is precisely what we are now experiencing. The more we have of this stuff, the more important it has become. It is a little unsettling, to be sure. To me, too. But it's not all bad, not by a long shot. In fact, relative to other systems, it's really quite fair.

THE PRICE IS RIGHT?

JACK GIBBONS

In the midst of the Great Depression, my mother would talk to me about the need to spend money, not just save it, in order to increase consumer demand so that people could become employed to provide goods and services. The only problem was that we had hardly any money and borrowing to spend for consumption was unthinkable. But the message was clear—it's patriotic to consume.

Later I read H. G. Wells's turn-of-the-century musings about future societies in which science and technology had advanced productivity so far that the labors of only a small portion of the population were sufficient to provide goods and services for all. In Wells's view the producers would become the privileged class, with everyone else relegated to a singular patriotic responsibility: to consume. An interesting turn of events, to be sure, but it made a point about the need to think about work and reward in an age of technology and knowledge-based economy.

More recently, the expansion of consumption has combined with the market system and open societies to drive down unit costs of goods and services to the point where yesterday's luxuries are today's affordable necessities. But rather than taking our gains in more leisure and contemplative activities we seem inextricably hitched to the treadmill of income production and insatiable consumerism, strongly abetted not by arguments of the Depression years but by commercial and even some religious figures.

What's wrong with this? I suggest that if prices were "right" we'd make wiser choices. But the private market cannot, or does not, charge for considerable "external" costs such as environmental damage, or intergenerational justice.

The results, as we move into the twenty-first century, are worrisome. Two centuries after Thomas Malthus's treatise on population, we need to recognize that we are headed into truly dangerous waters: too many people consuming too many resources on a finite planet.

The twenty-first century will be a century-long moment of truth for humankind. If we hope to continue human progress as the most extraordinary form of biological evolution we must transform our consumption passions into a sustainable rather than exponential form. And we must make a similar transition to a stabilized population. Technological progress can go only so far in enabling more people to consume more goods while staying on a sustainable course. Without a change in direction, as an old Chinese statement goes, "We're very likely to end up where we are headed."

What should be done? Julie Schor offers some interesting elements for a new policy of consumerism. I would take issue with only her first: a right to a decent standard of living.

My preference would be for rights of opportunity to earn a decent standard of living. We need safety nets, but I don't think we've arrived yet at H. G. Wells's visions of a future where people are paid simply to consume.

I offer a few suggestions for action:

1. *We need to get prices right*—to ensure that they reflect the true total cost of goods and services. As Schor points out, most consumer goods are underpriced. Whether by regulations (shadow price) or fees, we should pay the true cost of goods and services. Henry Caudill, Kentuckian lawyer and author, made a compelling case, for example, for stiff separations taxes to be placed on the sale of natural resources such as coal so that the wealth taken by this generation and denied future generations would be at least partly replaced by a different wealth—education and technology—for future generations.

2. *We should pay more attention to product labeling*—to make it trustworthy and meaningful. Recent progress in food labeling has been very helpful, and energy-efficiency labeling (like food, a federal requirement) helps achieve the economic assumption or goal that consumers exercise judgment when information is available. Remember the Sears labels of "good, better, best"? Or the Good Housekeeping Seal?

3. *We should give greater emphasis on truth in advertising*. The lure of easy access to credit cards, especially to the young and the poor, is destructive and relevant public policies need reform.

4. *More attention is needed in education and our churches and families to raising awareness of the value of nonmonetary things.* As one sage put it: "Being rich is having money; being wealthy is having time." As Schor points out, our opportunity is to stop marketplace bias against workers who wish to substitute some income for more time off from work.

"Think globally, act locally" is a phrase that merits more attention, and applies both in space and time. We all need, in our shrinking and accelerating world, to be more cognizant of the twenty-first-century imperative to stabilize population and transform the way we provide goods and services so that the system becomes more sustainable. This can be accomplished with the help of advanced technology used by thoughtful people. Otherwise we are destined to leave the planet a much poorer place—not an attractive goal for the human condition.

QUALITY OF LIFE

CLAIR BROWN

Juliet Schor's provocative and thoughtful call for a new politics of consumption raises important issues about why Americans are obsessed by private consumption and how this affection for commodities is adversely affecting our lives. I agree with much of her analysis, including her indictment of modern economic thinking about consumption. Where I part company is with her claim that the problems of consumption are more urgent now because materialistic pressures have increased over earlier periods. Though this claim about growing pressures is not necessary for her critique of consumerism, it may lead her to underestimate the difficulty of creating an effective politics of consumption.

The "positional treadmill" that Schor describes is a major force behind our obsession with private consumption. But my research on American standards of living does not find an accelerating treadmill. It indicates instead that working families dramatically increased their spending on status consumption as a proportion of their budgets between 1950 and 1973, but increased it only slightly between 1973 and 1988.[1] I categorized families as laborers (unskilled and service), wage earners (semiskilled and skilled), and salaried (professional and managerial not self-employed). I found that laborer families increased the proportion spent on status from 2 percent of their budget in 1950 to 15 percent in 1973, and then to 21 percent in 1988. The story with salaried families was similar: they increased their status consumption from 18 percent of their budget in 1950 to 27 percent in 1973, and then to 31 percent in 1988. Wage earners' families increased the proportion spent on status from 10 percent of their budget in 1950 to 19 percent in 1973, and then to 22 percent in 1988. Expenditures for variety or comfort consumption remained fairly constant over this period: roughly 10 percent of the budget for laborer families and 25 percent for wage earner and salaried families.

Two important intellectual shifts over the 1950–88 period reinforced the emphasis on private consumption. In consumption theory, Milton Friedman's *permanent income hypothesis*—that family consumption is a constant portion of expected lifetime income—displaced James Duesenberry's *relative income hypothesis*—that consumption depends in part on income relative to other families—as a way of understanding a family's economic position. Lifetime income, which is an absolute measure, determined a family's position; relative income (and differences across families) no longer mattered. Second, the emphasis on performance pay in the 1980s and 1990s—the idea that compensation should reflect measured individual performance—focused attention on individual contributions and served as the justification for rising inequality, even though the "quality" differences across individuals remained unobservable. Together, permanent consumption and performance pay meant that economic outcomes reflected individual choice and value-added. Ideas about economic opportunity, about access to good and bad jobs, or about bargaining power and rent sharing tended to drop from sight. And if your income reflects your choices and contributions, rather than your inherited advantages or your bargaining power, then conspicuous consumption is a way to show your value to society.

But even if Schor is wrong in her claim that social pressures to consume have increased, she is right that the *problem* of consumption has become more urgent, and for the reasons she states: increasingly detrimental outcomes to our environment and our communities, and the need to improve living standards in the developing world. Any movement to restore a balanced use of resources globally and to improve the quality of life in the United States must challenge the lifestyles of working- and middle-class families, in addition to the rich. We may in the end decide that the typical "meager livelihoods" of working families are not inadequate in an egalitarian society that has more public goods, leisure time, and security.

Let me put this point about adequacy in perspective. In 1988, typical working families with incomes between $30,000 and $50,000 (in 1998 dollars)[2] owned their homes, had air-conditioning, owned at least one car, spent a quarter of their food budget away from home, and went on 1.5 vacations annually that cost $655 each (out of $3,535 spent on leisure activities). If we look more closely, we find that they spent $1,140 yearly on a variety of household furnishings such as sofas, refrigerators, and decorative items, and another $1,635 on household operations including telephone service, gardening, and cleaning supplies. At the same time, they were eating too much sugar, fat, protein, and salt as they consumed junk food and sodas and too few vitamins.[3] From a world viewpoint or a historical viewpoint, these families were not living a meager lifestyle; yet in modern-day America, thoughtful commentators find it lacking.

Socially defining a comfortable lifestyle is extremely controversial across the political spectrum. Reversing the obsession for higher incomes so families can buy more is an unpopular proposition that goes against the heart of American culture. In this regard, the 1990s does not deviate at all from previous decades: in the 1920s, the Lynds' study of Middletown lamented "Why did they work so hard?"

The crucial issue is: what constitutes the quality of life? Schor is correct to pull us back to a discussion about what absolute level of private consumption provides the resource basis for a meaningful life so that we can focus on improving the quality of life globally. Judging by our history, affluence, and inequality, I predict it will be a rancorous discussion.

THE PERSONAL LEVEL

BETSY TAYLOR

Americans are consuming like there may be no tomorrow. The dominance of consumerism is arguably more pervasive now than it has been at any time in human history. Our most popular national pastime is watching television, followed closely by recreational shopping. The United States has the highest per capita consumption rate in the industrial world. While our material gains have improved the quality of life in some notable ways, there are many hidden costs to our "more is better" definition of the American dream. Juliet Schor is one of the few intellectuals to rigorously examine these costs. Her call for a new politics of consumption warrants serious debate.

Schor does an excellent job of exposing the underbelly of our consumerist culture. Her analytic work, including her recent book, *The Overspent American,* focuses primarily on how our work-and-spend lifestyles undermine the quality of our lives. In the chase for more, Americans are working longer hours and racking up more debt while finding fewer hours to enjoy their material acquisitions. Schor's research also reveals a troubling new trend: our collective tendency to always want much more than we have. In a culture that reveres Bill Gates, the rising stock market, and status goods, people are no longer comparing themselves with the textbook Joneses, but rather with the wealthy celebrities they see on television. For many, this never-ending expansion of wants leads to conspicuous consumption, psychological stress, and a preoccupation with meeting nonmaterial needs materially.

In her essay, Schor points to the other hidden costs of excessive consumerism. Perhaps most troubling, though—and something Schor might have addressed in greater detail—is the environmental damage wreaked by American consumption. With less than 5 percent of the world's population, the United States consumes nearly 30 percent of global resources. Since 1940, Americans alone have used up as large a share of Earth's mineral resources as have all previous humans put together. Per person, we use twice as much energy and generate more than twice as much garbage as the average European. The typical American discards nearly a ton of trash per year. We consume 40 percent of the world's gasoline and own 32 percent of the world's cars. The average new house built in the United States has doubled in size since 1970. Two thirds of those houses have two-car garages. To offer some perspective, scientists recently issued a study for the Earth Council indicating that if everyone on Earth consumed as the average North American does, we would need four extra planets to supply the resources and absorb the waste.

What does this mean for the environment? Every product comes from Earth and returns to it. To produce our cars, houses, hamburgers, televisions, sneakers, newspapers, and thousands upon thousands of other consumer items, we rely on chains of production that stretch around the globe. The unintended consequences of these chains include global warming, rapid deforestation, the depletion of over 25 percent of the world's fish stocks, and the permanent loss of hundreds of plant and animal species, including the very real possibility of losing all large mammals in the wild within the next fifty years.

Along with taking a heavy toll on our quality of life and the planet, consumerism is also placing tremendous pressure on low-income families. The American preoccupation with acquisition afflicts the rich and poor alike. And our collective fixation on keeping up with commercial consumerist norms often wreaks havoc on those in low-income communities and exacerbates the growing gap between the rich and poor. Few would dispute that those living on the economic margins need more material goods. But the culture of consumerism weighs heavily on the 35 million Americans living below the poverty line. The relentless marketing of status footwear, high-cost fashion, tobacco, and alcohol to low-income neighborhoods is one of the most pernicious aspects of consumer culture. The politics that Schor describes would challenge a culture that encourages people to define themselves through their stuff and would especially support and empower young Americans who feel enormous pressure to acquire things as the only avenue for gaining love, respect, and a sense of belonging.

Schor describes seven basic elements to a new "politics of consumption." Her elements, or guiding principles for an emerging movement, invite a fusion of those working for justice with those working for environmental sustainability. Her first principle, the right to a decent standard of living, requires affluent environmentalists and progressives to look anew at what structures must be put in place to ensure a level of safety and security for all Americans. If people don't feel safer—about the future and about their kids—they can't entertain the deeper moral and environmental question "How much is enough?" Schor does not specify the components necessary to give people greater security, but the litany of real needs is well known: affordable housing, quality health care, living-wage jobs, medical care in old age, funds for retirement, and affordable college education for children. People feel alone. It's hard to stop the chase for money, if not stuff, when you feel no support structures. Unless progressives reembrace these concerns, those in poor and middle-class families will have difficulty connecting with Schor's politics. Too many progressives have become seduced by the culture of desire: we, too, look up instead of down. We spend too much time in isolation from those living in poverty. With some exceptions, we have lost our edge. Perhaps we are just too comfortable. Perhaps this is unavoidable in a noisy culture that bombards us with three thousand commercial messages a day.

Schor's other principles ring true. Millions of Americans obviously share her call for more fun, less stuff. Millions are opting to downshift, choosing to make less money in search of more time. A growing number of people also affirm her call for responsible consumption, a call for a much higher consciousness about the environmental and human costs of each consumer decision we make. Her call to democratize consumer markets seems a bit naïve since humans have probably always sought to define themselves in part through their stuff. But in an age of excessive materialism, the times may be ripe to challenge the dominant ethos. Perhaps we can make it cool to shun fashion and footgear with corporate logos and redefine hip as simple, real, and noncommercial.

Her fifth principle taps into growing opposition to globalization and a dismaying recognition that Bangkok and New York look increasingly the same. After two decades of megamergers and five years of intense globalization, the homogenization of retail environments is destroying local businesses and cultures. A recommitment to local economies, independent small businesses, and consumer products that are locally designed and produced could be good for jobs, the environment, and cultural diversity.

The only principle that seems missing to me is one that goes to the heart of our values. Progressives tend to squirm when encouraged to examine values at a personal level. We want to change the system yet we remain uncomfortable with "soft" discussions of individual transformation. But there is a huge churning under way about values, purpose, and spirit. Progressives can dogmatically dismiss these forces as elements of religious dogmatism or New Age narcissism, or they can connect with this churning. I would argue that a politics of consumption—and we need a better name for this—should include guiding principles of humility and compassion. Humility and awe in surrendering to the "not knowing" about the cosmology of things, coupled with an affirmation of all those who hunger to experience the Light, however one defines that. We need a politics that embraces compassion for Earth, for each other as individuals of equal human value, and especially for children who will inherit the future. Can we not come together with new energy, passion, and vision, combining forces for justice and sustainability with the hunger for rekindled spirits? Does a critique of consumer culture open up this discussion in new and encouraging ways? Schor argues that it does. I am persuaded that she is on to something.

POSTMODERN MARKETS

DOUGLAS B. HOLT

Juliet Schor perceptively describes a complex set of social problems that demand political remedy. But I disagree with her analysis of the new consumerism and, thus, with her proposed remedies.

Analytically, Schor argues that dramatic increases in economic inequality have combined with increasing social comparisons with upscale reference groups in the mass media to produce an intensive quest for upper-middle-class status goods. Widespread participation in this inflated status game has socially destructive results, including environmental degradation, shrinking public provisioning, and an "aspirational gap"—with personal debt spiraling up and personal happiness spiraling down.

As to remedies, Schor's proposals aim to stem both competitive consumption and its harmful welfare effects. She wants a consumer movement that promotes family, religious, communal, egalitarian, and environmental values rather than status competition. She also calls for taxes on status goods, green taxes and subsidies, and tighter regulations on credit and advertising.

The Postmodern Market

While I share many of Schor's personal commitments, I don't think her agenda will work as intended because she has misidentified the basic mechanisms that generate over-consumption and its attendant consequences. What is now driving consumption is not *upscale emulation,* but, in a word, *differentiation.*

The contemporary market—let's call it the "postmodern market"—depends increasingly upon two strategies to increase sales and profits. First, areas of social life that traditionally fell outside the market—health care, education, prisons, religion, the arts, poverty, the environment, caring for the elderly and the dead—are now being brought into the market. Second, consumer identities are being fragmented, proliferated, recombined, and turned into salable goods. Thus, transnational companies compete on how quickly and effectively they can create markets out of new styles, meanings, and experiences produced in public culture. For example, Nike has abandoned the core principle of modern marketing, which advises companies to weave into their advertising only those elements of public culture that are consistent with the distinctive meanings of the brand. Instead, Nike is bent upon attaching the "swoosh" logo to *any* person, place, or thing that achieves recognition in the popular cultural world of sports. Monopolizing the public channels of meaning creation—grabbing the latest public fashion—is becoming more important than monopolizing particular meanings.

The culture that supports these postmodern market conditions is premised upon an extreme version of consumer sovereignty. The "good life" is not a matter of having a well-defined list of status goods now possessed by wealthy television personalities. Instead, it is an open-ended project of self-creation. The idea is to circulate continually through new experiences, things, and meanings, to play with different identities by consuming the goods and services associated with those identities. The market promotes a sense of freedom from constraint, an ultimate individuality through commodities. Environmental degradation, the personal debt crisis, and private provisioning are the unhappy results of these unnatural beginnings. As desires become more dynamic and promiscuous, consumption levels soar. Impossibly high incomes (or loads of debt) seem absolutely necessary, but not because we aspire to mimic the status goods of the upper middle class as seen on television. Rather, fountains of money are needed to participate in the postmodern version of the "good life," in which one pursues enhanced experiences and multiple lifestyles by purchasing their ever-changing props.

If I'm right that postmodern market conditions lead to overconsumption problems, then a different kind of political intervention than the "new politics of consumption" is required. To see why, let's suppose that Schor's proposals were instituted. What social changes would result? My analysis suggests the following:

1. *Social class is but one of many identities that the market promotes.* Thus, if status competition were completely shut down, the market would effortlessly redirect that fraction of market activity devoted to status competition to other kinds of self-definition.

2. *The market would find the nonstatus values that Schor's agenda encourages and turn them into salable goods.* For example, the communitarian lifestyle (Disney's Rockwellian Celebration, Florida), the progressive lifestyle (Benetton, the Body Shop, Working Assets), the green lifestyle (the Nature Company, Smith & Hawken, Ben & Jerry's). Challenges to the market from alternative lifestyles can be turned into more grist for the postmodern market.

3. *The new politics of consumption agenda would not impact social inequality.* Schor assumes that there is a fixed set of "positional goods" that are used to convey status. Yet one of Bourdieu's most forceful arguments is that social distinction is not produced by a consensual set of status goods, but by socially endowed sensibilities that are expressed through acts of consumption. Historians and sociologists have shown conclusively that status consumption is extremely dynamic, moving easily across goods and categories. So, even if it were possible to limit the consumption of particular goods that are now status symbols, status competition would simply shift to other goods and activities.

A Political Response

If the cause of overconsumption problems is located in the postmodern organization of the market, challenges must aim at market structure, in particular at the processes through which the market recycles public culture as commodities, not the specific goods and services currently for sale. The market will cease to promote postmodern consumer culture only when this strategy becomes more difficult and less profitable (or, alternatively, higher profits are to be had from new strategies). For example, "cultural pilfering" taxes on advertising, sponsorships, tie-in promotions, and public relations expenses would slow the proliferation of commercialized culture. Or, perhaps the process could be hampered by limiting commercial access to the mass media and legislating in favor of more public noncommercial media outlets and fewer private ones.[1]

Intervening with market structure rather than market content is also politically preferable. Though Schor understands the elitist, antidemocratic problems inherent in legislating how people should consume, she can't avoid proposals that dictate consumption patterns because her analysis focuses on commercial content. For example, she calls for legislation favoring mom-and-pop retailers over chains. In my research, I've found that working-class people absolutely depend upon Wal-Mart, Kmart, and JCPenney for inexpensive merchandise of reasonable quality and look forward with great enthusiasm to a celebratory meal at Red Lobster and shopping trips to the local outlet mall. Is it appropriate to discourage these practices?

We also need a strategy for mobilizing consumers, but one based upon different organizing principles from Schor's. To deflate the motivating force of postmodern consumer culture requires a collective understanding of the linkages between nomadic consumer desires, recombinant consumer identities, and the structure of the postmodern market. As the troubles spawned by the postmodern market continue to grow—and Schor's figures on credit card debt suggest that the strategy is approaching its limit—it is crucial to anticipate ways to frame this critique of consumerism in a manner that will resonate with a broad audience. Paradoxically, an anti-consumerism movement must adopt sophisticated marketing techniques to have any hope of resonating with people for whom commercial rhetoric has become the dominant vernacular of social life.

A NEW PURITANISM?

CRAIG J. THOMPSON

Juliet Schor rightly chastises conventional economic theory for its narrow, rationalistic understanding of consumer preferences. As an alternative, she sketches a sociological model of consumption, in which consumers go in for up-scale emulation and endlessly ratchet up their competitive consumption.

Schor's "status game" analysis conveys important insights and is an improvement over the economistic alternative. But applause does not foster discussion, so I propose here to focus on two related points of disagreement: first, Schor is insufficiently attentive to the cultural complexity of consumption; second, her critique of consumption resonates with a puritanical moralism that demonizes consumption as a source of enervation and irrational excess.

1. *Culture and consumption.* An extensive body of consumer studies has documented that many central aspects of both personal and collective identity are created, maintained, and transformed through consumption.[1] Personal enrichment and communal affiliation do not exist outside of consumption or necessarily in opposition to it. The status game critique of consumption is most compelling when one accepts the romantic view that individuals harbor an au-

thentic self that can only be distorted by the seductions of consumer culture. It is less compelling when identity is taken to be socially constructed. From this perspective, consumer culture provides symbolic tools for constructing and reconstructing identity through self-defining leisure practices. (Am I, for example, a runner, couch potato, classical pianist, foreign film aficionado, or perhaps some combination?) Consumption also links individuals together. On a small scale, consider the social bonds enacted through the ritual sharing of a meal or gift exchange. On larger scale, think of youth-oriented "rave" cultures, Harley-Davidson enthusiasts, or the virtual communities coalescing around popular culture entertainment (for example, the resurgent *Star Wars* community). Accordingly, an effective politics of consumption must move beyond a critique of materialism and address the deep connections between personal and communal identity and consumption practices.

For Schor the conspicuous act of materially "keeping up with the Joneses" is the linchpin of contemporary consumption. But this formulation is in some ways behind the postmodern times. Consumers are already pursuing an improved quality of life rather than greater quantity of stuff, and consumer culture is right there selling "it" to them with great skill and alacrity. Whether in the form of travel or museum patronage, self-enriching leisure activities are fundamentally embedded in marketing techniques and the exigencies of consumer culture. Furthermore, nothing is more heavily marketed than spiritual development: the "new age" industry, the mass-marketed quasi-Eastern mysticism espoused by Deepak Chopra, and religious experience (marketing is not just for televangelism anymore) are just a few of the "spiritual goods" available on the market. Indeed, postmodern consumer culture has been characterized as a post-materialist "economy of signs," in which self-enhancement and even spiritual epiphany are dominant consumer motivations. Of course, material goods still carry much symbolic currency, but consumption practices that enable individuals to create a "mindful," "centered," "authentic" identity, immune to "other-directed" pressures, are now important markers of social status. An effective politics of consumption must address this essential element of postmodern consumer culture.

Reducing consumption to an unreflective, Veblenesque status game also elides the role of consumption in negotiating political and cultural ideas and sensibilities. Thus, consider the role of popular culture as a domain of expression and protest for those on the socioeconomic margins and other countercultural groups:[2] Chuck D said that rap music is the "black CNN." Yes, these expressions of cultural resistance have been routinely co-opted by the market.[3] Still, consumer culture gives expression to a multitude of meanings, values, and social interests. And even when these countercultural motifs enter the mainstream, they carry the potential for subtle forms of social change. Once-marginal ideas about environmentalism and naturalism, for example, have fostered an increasingly critical stance toward a status-chasing, materialistic lifestyle and the "depthless" world of mass-produced goods, glamorizing advertising pitches, home shopping networks, and dizzyingly garish shopping malls.

2. *Puritanism.* Veblen is usually credited with the original insight into the dire consequences of conspicuous consumption. But his oh-so-seminal account tapped into a broader range of fin de siècle anxieties about the detrimental effects of modern civilization upon masculinity. The Victorian "cult of domesticity," which fostered the cultural link between consumption and femininity, was widely criticized as emasculating, and thus threatening the moral fiber (as well as the bodies) of the next generation of patriarchs. The contemporary manifestation of this historical legacy is the view of consumption as a wanton and scandalously profane activity that impedes the attainment of a higher moral-spiritual plane. If real, deep, genuine, higher human needs could triumph over artificial consumer desires, "the good society" would lie within reach.

What's the problem with this despairingly disparaging view of consumption? For starters, consumer culture has been uniquely attuned to the social positions of women and their culturally constructed feminist aesthetic.[4] The moral critique of consumerism has an inescapably patriarchal background: it is steeped in a phobia of feminization and an infatuation with puritanical asceticism. It effects a rejection of the sensual and emotive aspects of human experience and an extreme suspicion of "unproductive" pleasures.

Consumption is dangerous precisely because it resists this rationalized, puritanical, patriarchal construction of the perfect society. That actual consumer behavior does not correspond even a little bit to the "rational man" model so lionized by conventional economists is not just a theoretical oversight but the very point. Consumer behavior has always been an inexplicable misbehavior for those who envision a rational social order: it is too emotive, irrational, and impelled by desires for pleasure and baroque excess—"why can't a consumer be more like a rational man?"

Rather than extolling the middle class to "resist" the seductive enticements of the market-place and consume more autonomously and rationally, perhaps we should abandon this self-disciplining, rationalist discourse altogether. Such abandonment need not lead to an even greater preoccupation with consumption. An irony not to be overlooked is that this pervasive moralistic critique of consumption has been the historical concomitant to the explosive increase in materialism. Perhaps the never-ending cycle of work-spend and the ceaseless quest for "new things" has less to do with a desire to "keep up with the Joneses" than a deeply internalized inhibition against pleasure.[5]

So, perhaps a radical politics of consumption should argue for getting more pleasure out of consumption, rather than repackaging the age-old admonition that individuals seek "true" fulfillment by escaping the flesh, or mortifying it. Schor makes the cogent point that everyone in the advertising industry knows that consumers are not rational, utility maximizers. They also know that "sex sells." Though it is tempting to say that it sells "despite our puritanical view of sexuality," the truth may be that it sells "because of our puritanical view of sexuality." Could it be that insatiable materialistic desires and the undeniable ecological dangers posed by overconsumption are equally dependent on a puritanical rendering of consumer pleasure as a moral danger— and therefore as worthy of our devotion?

TOO MUCH ECONOMICS

MICHÈLE LAMONT AND VIRÁG MOLNÁR

In *The Morality of Spending,* Daniel Horowitz shows that generations of American social critics have addressed the perils of changing patterns of consumption.[1] These critics, according to Horowitz, understood the consequences of these patterns but were limited in their vision of the social meaning of consumption by their moralistic outlooks. Juliet Schor's essay offers well-intentioned suggestions about how to revive this tradition of social criticism. But her economistic point of departure severely constrains her own alternative.

To be sure, Schor's economic perspective conveys important insights. She focuses our attention on the tension between a growing polarization of income and the upscaling of consumption in American society: as desires grow, fewer people have the means to afford what they desire; the result is a general decline in Americans' sense of well-being. The Good Life is increasingly defined in terms of upper-middle-class standards, which can be achieved by but a few. The cost of failing is rising, at least in psychological terms.

This starting point is extremely fruitful and addresses what we consider to be one of the main conundrums of contemporary American society: with social citizenship defined in terms of consumption, and with disposable income rising for few and falling for many, how can the majority of the population maintain a sense of self-worth? This problem is becoming more salient not only in the United States, but all over the world, as both the market and, more broadly, neoliberalism become the dominant organizing principles of social life.

Schor's past and current writings have appeal largely because she takes as a point of departure the very economic theory that has become commonsense knowledge in contemporary American society. What she writes resonates with the folk theories of the "average educated reader" about how the world works. But economic theory is also the source of the main shortcomings of her contribution—shortcomings that, in our view, plague the details of her diagnosis and solution. Her challenge to consumer society does not go beyond the classical critique of the economic theory of consumer behavior.[2] This limitation prevents her from fully comprehending the complex meanings that various groups attribute to consumption. Paradoxically, it also prevents her from offering solutions that truly transcend the idea that "money is a key to happiness." Finally, her understanding of the role of consumer movements, and of progressive intellectuals in them, is marred by an unconvincing voluntarism.

Schor criticizes the economic theory of consumption for assuming, for example, that consumers are rational. She offers rich evidence that this and other assumptions are unfounded. However, her description of what guides consumption is generally framed in individual terms. The implicit model she uses remains an economic one, that of a single individual entering a shopping mall and *choosing* among goods to maximize the investment of his or her resources, with the primary goal of accumulating goods to gain status. The definition of status itself is not treated as a problem and social relations enter the equation only through the determination of individual preferences (via the impact of reference groups).

An alternative, more cultural model would frame consumption as a social act: shopping, for example, is often done with a friend or family member and with someone else's needs in mind.[3] And it would not define consumption in opposition to leisure, as shopping itself is often considered a pastime. Finally, it would examine the full range of definitions of status and worth that people adopt, and their articulation with socioeconomic status in particular.

The dominance of an economic model in Schor's argument is also apparent in her failure to systematically differentiate between the meanings given to consumption by members of different classes and races. Her many examples privilege a specific upper-middle-class stance by claiming that conspicuous consumption is primary: as always, Newton prevails over Roxbury. But to address the upscaling of needs, one should differentiate carefully among the understandings of consumption by upper-middle-class, working-class, and poor people. For this last group, meeting basic needs is often primary. For the American working class, quality of life is often defined in terms of the defense of personal integrity and dignity, as well as in terms of consumption.[4] For the upper middle class, the goal of maximizing one's socioeconomic status de facto frequently goes hand in hand with the construction of a morally meaningful life and the pursuit of self-actualization. Finally, for blacks as opposed to whites, consumption is often the key to a positive collective identity.[5] Moreover, the logic of conspicuous consumption is different for black urban youths and residents of Manhattan's Upper East Side. Marketing specialists have identified the urban youth market as one of the fastest-growing market segments, and these consumers do not emulate the taste of the white upper middle class, while Schor implies that everyone emulates this group.[6]

The impact of economic theory on Schor's thinking is also apparent in the alternative she offers. She proposes to replace an exclusive focus on individual private consumption with a focus on spending *differently* (that is, by investing in public consumption, buying free time, and saving). However, interviews suggest that individuals who strive to keep the logic of profit and social-position maximization from dominating their lives do so less by finding new ways to spend and by reducing the importance of spending in their lives than by centering their attention on other spheres and activities: intimacy, creativity, morality, religion, education, and the arts, for example.[7] This does not mean that consumption is peripheral to people's identity. But how one relates to what one consumes is as important as what one consumes. In other words, the cultural framing of consumption is not as stable as Schor implies; in fact, the spending patterns of the upper middle class have less legitimacy than she grants them, as goods are always multivocal, even for low-status groups.

Finally, Schor invites us to rejuvenate consumer movements by developing a "new politics of consumption" that aims in part at encouraging people to "welcome initiatives that reduce the pressure they feel to keep up with rising standards." An unrepentant voluntarism underlies this proposal. Schor emphasizes changes in private consumption practices—personal restraints—as the solution to our conundrum.[8] Taxing luxury products is also offered as a viable strategy. Instead, we submit that change is more likely to emerge from gaining a better understanding of how people develop a sense of self-worth and define a worthy life, and using that understanding to sharpen the messages progressive social movements offer. Well-intentioned scholars such as Schor need to frame alternatives to market-driven lives by looking beyond consumption. Indeed, dignity, personal integrity, and self-actualization are often achieved through meaningful relationships with others, instead of through things. If social membership is so often defined by consumption in American society, alternative bases of membership remain available and must be explored.

These criticisms should not distract from the importance of Schor's contribution in alerting us to the urgency of the situation: she is among a handful of economists, including

Robert Frank, who attempt to bring back the social into the narrow path-dependent worldview of economists. But she clearly does not go far enough, and an effective tactician she is not. We may need a broader understanding of status to reach more convincing alternative paths to limitless emulation and conspicuous consumption.

LEISURE FOR ALL

LAWRENCE MISHEL, JARED BERNSTEIN,
AND JOHN SCHMITT

Juliet Schor is to be commended for tackling tough issues and pushing forward the frontiers of economic analysis. Such exploratory work necessarily moves the debate beyond established research and policy discussions, so there is no value in extensive quibbling over the evidence for or against her story line. Rather, we will identify areas of agreement and disagreement and areas where further exploration is needed to satisfy our skepticism.

Schor's main thesis is that we need a new "politics of consumption" because "the new consumerism" that arose in the 1980s—"a rapid escalation of desire and need"—is causing stress, harming the environment, and weakening the public sector.

We agree about the importance of a vision focused on "quality of life" rather than "quantity of stuff." So in our work at the Economic Policy Institute,[1] we stress changes in "living standards" rather than income per se. Although we see a strong connection between improved living standards and higher income, we know that income is not a complete measure of "economic well-being," let alone a complete measure of living standards or quality of life. And we certainly agree that justice requires a vastly more equal distribution of income, wealth, and power, both domestically and globally.

We agree, too, that the typical American (by which we mean the median household or family) "finds it harder to achieve a satisfying standard of living than did the average American twenty-five years ago." Incomes have been relatively stagnant since 1973 despite a greater share of family members working, and working more hours annually, in the paid labor force. This stagnation is the result of slow productivity growth and a phenomenal growth in income inequality. These income trends, along with the erosion of employer-provided pension and health insurance coverage and high involuntary job displacement, have induced stress and insecurity, exacerbated crime, and widened a maldistribution of health outcomes. Some of these trends have ameliorated in the period of low unemployment since 1996, but we fear they will return as unemployment returns to more familiar levels.

The causes of the productivity slowdown are not well known but the growth of income inequality has been primarily driven by the growing inequality of hourly wages. Wage inequality, in turn, has been driven by a redistribution of power achieved through such laissez-faire policies as globalization (foreign investment, trade, and the sensitive issue of immigration), deregulation, deunionization, a weakened social safety net, and a lower minimum wage in the context of relatively high unemployment (especially in the early 1980s, when much of this redistribution took place). A related phenomenon has been a significant redistribution of income from wage to capital (profit and interest) income.

We agree with Schor that current policies and market forces do not adequately protect the environment or adequately support public investment (infrastructure, education) or social insurance and transfers. The public sector, "government," has been under a widespread, intensive assault for several decades now. However, we would not want to overdramatize the outcome of this struggle, as the public sector's share of national resources has remained relatively constant. Moreover, the attack on government is the product of many factors, including a general decline in voters' faith in the effectiveness of government, stagnant pretax incomes (making taxes more of an issue), and an aggressive ideological and policy assault from business and the well-off (who need fewer public services). We disagree with Schor in that we do not see a role for a new consumer mentality, independent of the factors just described, leading to the squeeze on government and a shift in spending from public to private goods. It is notable that the GOP has gotten little political traction for its tax-cut agenda in the last few years as incomes and wages have been rising across the board.

It is also hard to see a new consumerism as responsible for the loss of leisure. We agree that there has been such a loss. But it is principally driven by more women working, and more women working full-year and full-time. It does not reflect a general rise in average weekly hours, as we would expect if a new consumerist urge to spend was driving leisure down. This greater (paid) work effort is part of a decades-long increase in women's labor force participation, reinforced by feminism and male wage deterioration. The growth in women's paid work hours has been greatest among lower- and middle-income families and not among the well-off.[2] (We suspect this does not correspond to a "new consumerism," since these are the families where male wages and family incomes have fared worst. In fact, in the absence of wives' increased contributions, the income of these families would have fallen, instead of merely stagnating.)

Nor is it clear to us that the leisure problem is *primarily* due to employers' blocking options of workers—failing to provide a sufficiently flexible range of labor/leisure packages. True, employer policies do not appropriately correspond to the preferences of workers regarding the extent or timing of work. Nevertheless, there does seem to us to be a basic American cultural preference for income over leisure (certainly relative to Europe), as witnessed by the eagerness for overtime and the willingness of workers to accept less paid time off (for example, vacations) rather than wage reductions during concession bargaining in the 1980s. So, it is values and economics at work here.

In some cases, our response to Schor's arguments is more simply skeptical (or perhaps not adequately informed). One is that "consumption is part of the problem," meaning that the new consumerism is an independent force exacerbating inequalities. We presume that this notion goes beyond the obvious point that a maldistribution of power, wealth, and income leads to a maldistribution in consumption, and that when the well-off gain excessively, one finds ugly, excessive spending. It is also true that vast inequalities exacerbate the risks in not clinging to or getting one's progeny onto the same or higher rung of the social ladder. But we need to hear more about how materialistic consumer attitudes, independent of income and wealth, affect inequalities. We are also dubious that more income, once above the poverty level, "is relatively unimportant in affecting well-being," or that economic growth over the last few decades is associated with *declines* in well-being.

We are also skeptical that there is a set of consumer values, called "new consumerism," that arose in the 1980s and that have a qualitatively and quantitatively different impact on the economy. We note that this has been a period of historically *slow* consumption growth in the United States and other advanced countries (except among the very well-off in the United States).

Schor usefully asks whether those of us who emphasize renewing growth and greater equity would find achieving a $50,000 income for the typical family sufficient, or is it necessary to go toward $100,000? Where is the end of this process? she asks. Fair enough. The answer is "it depends." If income growth comes from people working much longer and harder, the gains may well not be worth the effort. But if productivity growth (defined as getting more from the same human and material inputs) fuels income growth, then there is no problem with expanding income or the standard of adequate income. It is similar with growth that results from enhanced human skills or better equipment. Nor are we sure it is problematic if the share of the population working continues to increase. Furthermore, it is not obvious that we face resource constraints that require us to limit, rather than to shape, growth. Environmentally destructive growth where the vast majority do not see income growth is clearly problematic. But that hardly describes all economic growth.

We too are troubled by a phenomenon closely related to a "new consumerism." This is the continued "marketization" of all aspects of life—the extension of the market into new spheres. Commercialism runs amok, evidenced by commercials before you watch a movie (arriving in the late 1970s) and while you watch a movie (the ubiquitous practice of product placement). The amassing and use of personal data by marketeers not only erodes privacy but increasingly reduces us to a singular consumerist role. Making individuals subject to more risk via downsizing, via the privatization of social security, and via other erosions of the social safety net only compounds the problem.

Thus, there is a need to establish policies that "keep the market in its place" and that shape market practices (for example, employer policies) to accommodate personal lives and provide retirement, health, and other security.

Part of the struggle Schor calls for goes beyond this and

amounts to a "culture war" against materialism. To accomplish this, however, we will have to confront current and growing inequality, lest we ask those with a beleaguered living standard to reduce their consumption. But if combined with such confrontation, this culture war is well worth fighting: it would require that we articulate a vision founded on decent political values and establish mechanisms for the economy to reflect those values. Leisure for all!

3

REPLY

The contributors to this forum are an extraordinary group of people whose work I have long admired and learned from. I am honored by their willingness to comment on mine. These are exactly the kinds of discussions about consuming that we need. Has the postmodern marketplace of Holt, Thompson, and perhaps Lamont and Molnár vitiated the positional competitions of Schor, Brown, and Frank? Is the most urgent and profound failure of consumption its environmental impact (Gibbons and Taylor)? Or is inequality the larger problem (Mishel, Bernstein, and Schmitt)? Is there no middle ground between Twitchell's laissez-faire, celebratory attitude toward spending and his fear of the Consumer Police? These are vital analytical and political questions.

ANALYSIS

Let me begin with some questions about my analysis. Holt, Thompson, and Lamont and Molnár all argue that I have misinterpreted the current consumer culture. While they differ in their specifics, all three responses challenge the centrality that I accord to classic status competitions in my analysis of the growth of consumption. Holt and Thompson argue that a postmodern marketplace has replaced status seeking with (in Holt's words) an "open-ended project of self-creation," in which consumers do not aim to copy the wealthy but to reinvent themselves by consuming new things in new ways. Lamont and Molnár take the view that upper-middle-class white tastes are not widely shared across society, as in the classical status model.

Generally speaking, I think the postmodern perspective focuses excessively on youth, sub-cultures, new commodities, and "cutting edge" trends. And it takes too narrow and literal a view of how status operates. To focus the disagreement, however, I need to begin by correcting what strikes me as a mischaracterization of my view by Holt. I have never argued that there are *particular* or *fixed* status symbols. Status competition is a dynamic process, and particular status markers tend to lose prestige and value as they proliferate. (This, by the way, is what James Twitchell fails to mention in his comments about Uncle Louie's headstone. Twenty years from now, upscale home buyers will regard the slabs in the kitchen as tacky remnants of a previous generation's bad taste, and will spend large amounts of money ripping them out and replacing them.) What does remain fixed, and perhaps this is what Holt objects to, is that goods that are more socially visible in their use and possession tend to figure more prominently in competitions. So, for example, shoes, clothing, modes of transport, homes, and home decoration have historically been (and continue to be) central in status competitions. Even the most ardent advocate of the post-modern marketplace can hardly have missed the upscaling to luxury vehicles, designer clothing, and larger and more luxurious houses. If people are merely reinventing themselves, why do they typically turn to these visible symbols of their identities? At the same time, what Holt calls postmodern commodities (a weekend at Kripalu) are *also* implicated in this process. But this is nothing new: when consumption is rising, new commodities always enter the game. Perhaps I should mention that I have never argued for restricting particular commodities (except on grounds of environmental impacts), as some of these contributions suggest. My favorite type of anti-status tax is one that taxes higher-end versions of commodities more heavily. (And, for a final point on Holt, I certainly do not advocate taking away the opportunity for consumers to shop at cheaper outlets; my concern is with maintaining diversity in retailing. The question is whether or not Wal-Mart will be allowed to wipe out the individual proprietorships and smaller chains.)

Lamont and Molnár claim that I focus on Newton to the exclusion of Roxbury. It's a fair claim, about which I was quite explicit in my book (although not in my essay, given the brevity of the section on new consumerism). I do believe, however, that the differences Lamont and Molnár discuss (class and race, for example) have declined over the twentieth century. Roxbury and Newton youth are not simply the same, but with respect to *what consumers desire,* the trend has been toward more uniformity across groups. The fact that fashion innovations now go from Roxbury *to* Newton in no way invalidates this claim. Furthermore, status models do not require that all participants experience the game in the same way, only that different groups assign similar rankings to products. Inner-city youth and suburban stockbrokers both want BMWs, but it does not follow that they mean the same thing in both places.

Finally, if I am guilty of overemphasizing the classical status model, it is because I am responding to what strikes me as widespread hostility to this interpretation. I have always found this ironic, because it was just the moment when status competition intensified that the scholars began claiming that status seeking was dead. Ultimately, as Clair Brown reminds us, a large part of the answer to this question must be empirical. Her work on this question is a classic, and her findings on the 1973–88 period are a challenge to my interpretation. I wonder, though, if a shift from spending money on new products to spending money on upscale versions of existing products could account for her failure to see an increase in expenditures on status in the consumer expenditure data.

Some of the other responses raised issues of interpretation. I was a bit surprised that Robert Frank characterized me as favoring a "marketing explanation," in contrast to his account, which emphasizes changes in the income and wealth distribution. My *Overspent American* argues that the worsening distributions of income and wealth set off the current round of conspicuous consumption. Indeed, I believe this is one of the major points of similarity between Frank's account and mine. (The other is our common emphasis on the externalities associated with positional competitions, and our belief in the value of tax policy to dampen those competitions.) Where Frank and I differ is that he does not argue that the nature of reference group comparisons has changed, as I do. This is why television is important in my story: not because of advertising, but because of the bias in its programming toward affluent lifestyles and the impact that it has had on viewers' perceptions of reality—an impact that has grown with skyrocketing television viewing time over this period.

Finally, Mishel, Bernstein, and Schmitt offer an illuminating series of queries and cautionary notes. On a small point, I would say that the contribution of a "new consumerism" has precisely been to increase families' commitment to dual-earner households and full-time female labor force participation, rather than longer weekly hours. Many of the jobs that married women have been entering are salaried, and therefore longer weekly hours do not raise incomes. On the larger point of their skepticism about the value of raising consumerism as an issue in progressive politics, I understand it fully. It can be treacherous territory. But I would love to see their Economic Policy Institute do research on some of the basic questions that a consumer critique raises, such as the relations between income, free time, and quality of life, and the question of "limits to growth" raised by Taylor and Gibbons.

Politics

What about the politics of my position? To Craig Thompson's question about pleasure, I'm ambivalent. Of course, I'm all for pleasure. But I'd say pleasure is one of the things consumerism is pretty good at generating. If the response comes back that the market gives us only "false" short-term pleasures, I'd worry about falling into the trap of thinking that consuming is a world of artificial desire or low-brow amoralism. James Twitchell might want to tar me with that brush, but I've tried pretty hard to steer clear of a view with the improbable implication that consuming isn't satisfying. Mainly because I don't believe it.

I appreciate Taylor's pointing out that I gave short shrift to the environmental effects of consumption, and that those must play a central role in any political discourse of consumption. Coming to terms with our current destruction of the planetary ecology will be an important part of coming to a new set of values. In this regard, the suggestions of Jack Gibbons are extremely important—for better pricing, more truth in advertising, product labeling, and so forth.

Lamont and Molnár suggest that I'm too individualistic, economistic, and voluntaristic. On the first, one accusation is that I have an individualistic theory of shopping. Actually, I have no theory of shopping. I have a theory of spending, which people may do alone, or in company. My examples were merely that, for the purpose of showing what's wrong with the neoclassical view. I reject the charge of an individualist theory of spending because the action in my essay is all about people's attempts to connect to others, and the importance of social context. By the same token, in calling for a new politics of consumption, I am in no way arguing against nonmaterial meanings, values, and self-definition. Quite the opposite. My work emphasizes the importance of *time* in reproducing human relationships, and the trade-offs between free time and earning money (not consumption as an alternative to leisure). In this sense, I put myself very squarely in the camp that is questioning the relationship between income and happiness. On the question of excessive voluntarism, I would reply that my principles are a combination of structural change through policy, cultural change through individual and local collective action, and a larger national mobilization. I find it inconceivable that progress on these issues could be made without individual, collective, national, local, cultural, social, *and* economic change. Consumerism is just too powerful.

Finally, to James Twitchell: I have no beef with bad taste; it's the high-end stuff I'm worried about. You don't have to worry about my hassling the poor. Or even, for that matter, the rich. It's not particular commodities that worry me. It really is the "Big Points" that Twitchell doesn't want to talk about. Like Destroying the Planet. Or Not Having Time to Know Each Other. Or Not Having Decent News Because Advertisers Control Content.

Twitchell says at the end of his comments, "The more we

have of this stuff, the more important it has become. It is a little unsettling, to be sure. To me, too." After all his celebration of consumerism, it seems to worry Twitchell. And that means he is like me, and like most Americans.

NOTES

CLAIR BROWN / *Quality of Life*

1. Clair Brown, *American Standards of Living, 1918–1988* (Cambridge, Mass.: Blackwell, 1994), table 8.2.

2. This includes families with less than 10 percent of the average income for laborers to more than 10 percent of the average income for wage earners. The 1988 median household income was $37,500. Approximately 37 percent of families fell above and below this range. All dollar amounts are inflated to 1988 dollars. Ibid., pp. 370–71.

3. Ibid., ch. 7.

DOUGLAS B. HOLT / *Postmodern Markets*

1. Robert McChesney, "The Future of the Media," *Boston Review* (summer 1998): 4–8.

CRAIG J. THOMPSON / *A New Puritanism?*

1. See, for example, Eric J. Arnould and Linda L. Price, "'River Magic': Extraordinary Experience and the Service Encounter," *Journal of Consumer Research* 20 (June 1993): 24–46; and John Schouten and James McAlexander, "Subcultures of Consumption: An Ethnography of New Bikers," *Journal of Consumer Research* 22 (June 1995): 43–61.

2. See, for example, George Lipsitz, *Time Passages* (1990).

3. Of course, this "trickle-up" process of commodification also inspires new forms of cultural expression among countercultural groups struggling to distinguish themselves from the dominant culture.

4. See, among others, Rita Felski, *The Gender of Modernity* (Cam-

bridge, Mass.: Harvard University Press, 1993); and William Leach, *Land of Desire* (New York: Pantheon, 1991).

5. It's not just about sex. A mundane, if anecdotal, example should suffice to make the point. American consumer culture is notorious for its puritanical, self-abnegating, and hyper-controlling orientation toward food, and it is also a culture where junk food, sublimated advertising images of food erotica, obesity, and binge eating abound. In dramatic contrast, Continental cultures—the French being the exemplary case—view eating in highly sensual and social terms and, in general, have a far more relaxed and unproblematic relation to food.

MICHÈLE LAMONT AND VIRÁG MOLNÁR / *Too Much Economics*

1. Daniel Horowitz, *The Morality of Spending: Attitudes Toward the Consumer Society in America, 1875–1940* (Baltimore: Johns Hopkins University Press, 1985).

2. Schor constantly uses economistic jargon and metaphors in her essay. For instance, she writes about "markets for the alternatives to status or positional goods," the "market for public goods," the "market for time," the "underproduction of public goods," and the "underproduction of leisure."

3. See Daniel Miller, *The Theory of Shopping* (Ithaca, N.Y.: Cornell University Press, 1998).

4. Michèle Lamont, "Above 'People Above': Status and Worth Among White and Black Workers," in *The Cultural Territories of Race: Black and White Boundaries*, ed. Michèle Lamont (Chicago: University of Chicago Press and New York: Russell Sage Foundation, 1999).

5. See, for example, Virág Molnár and Michèle Lamont, "Social Categorization and Group Identification: How African Americans Shape Their Collective Identity Through Consumption," in *Interdisciplinary Approaches to Demand and Its Role in Innovation*, ed. Andrew McMeekin (Manchester: Manchester University Press, forthcoming).

6. Schor makes the same mistake as does Bourdieu in subsuming the tastes of the dominated groups to those of the dominant class. For instance, in her book *The Overspent American: The Unexpected Decline of Leisure* (New York: Basic Books, 1998), she suggests that Americans

mostly watch entertainment television that offers white upper-middle-class life as a model (for example, *E. R.*, *Friends*, and *L. A. Law*). In fact, the preferences of whites and blacks in television-watching preference have been diverging in recent years.

7. When Schor discusses alternative life strategies, she tends to downplay the noneconomic aspects of these activities. For instance, she describes work as an oppressive activity tied to moneymaking, while in fact it is often thought of as a realm of self-actualization. And though she writes that "large majorities hold ambivalent views about consumerism: they struggle with ongoing conflicts between materialism and an alternative set of values stressing family, religion, and community," she does not go beyond these mentions and explore the content of these values. Nor does she say how building intimacy, for example, could act as an alternative source of worth and/or status.

8. Schor advocates personal restraints as a form of "collective response" to consumption. Though she suggests it is wrongheaded to believe that "a pure act of will can resolve this issue," she does not provide any alternative to voluntarism.

LAWRENCE MISHEL, JARED BERNSTEIN, AND JOHN SCHMITT / *Leisure for All*

1. See Lawrence Mishel, Jared Bernstein, and John Schmitt, *The State of Working America, 1998–99,* (an Economic Policy Institute book) (Ithaca, N.Y.: Cornell University Press, 1998).

2. Ibid., table 1.17.

ABOUT THE CONTRIBUTORS

CLAIR BROWN is professor of economics at the University of California, Berkeley, where she directs the Center for Work, Technology, and Society.

ROBERT H. FRANK is Goldwin Smith Professor of Economics, Ethics, and Public Policy at Cornell University. He is the author, most recently, of *Luxury Fever.*

JACK GIBBONS is senior fellow at the National Academy of Engineering in Washington, D.C., and special adviser for science and technology to the State Department.

DOUGLAS B. HOLT is assistant professor of advertising at the University of Illinois at Urbana-Champaign.

MICHÈLE LAMONT is associate professor of sociology at Princeton University. Her most recent book is *The Cultural Territories of Race: Black and White Boundaries.*

LAWRENCE MISHEL, JARED BERNSTEIN, and JOHN SCHMITT are economists at the Economic Policy Institute in Washington, D.C., and co-authors of *The State of Working America, 1998–99.*

VIRÁG MOLNÁR is a graduate student in the department of sociology at Princeton University.

JULIET SCHOR teaches at Harvard University and is author, most recently, of *The Overspent American: The Unexpected Decline of Leisure.*

BETSY TAYLOR is executive director of the Center for a New American Dream, http://www.newdream.org.

CRAIG J. THOMPSON is associate professor of marketing at the University of Wisconsin, Madison.

JAMES B. TWITCHELL, professor of English at the University of Florida, is the author, most recently, of *Lead Us into Temptation: The Triumph of American Materialism.*